I0620036

Hope That Never Fades
Devotional

Tiaina Doughty

Hope That Never Fades
Devotional

Publisher: Tiaina Doughty

Copyright © 2024 Tiaina Doughty
All rights reserved. No part of this book may be used or reproduced in any manner without written permission from the author except for the use of a brief quotation in a book review or scholarly journal.

ISBN: 979-8-218-45100-4

Book and Cover Design by Williams DocuPrep
www.williamsdocuprep.com

Thank You

Thank you for your purchase of Hope That Never Fades. Remember that wherever you go, God is there. You are never alone. Jesus wants each of us to know and have a personal relationship with Him for ourselves. No matter who leaves your life, hold on to the truth that God is always with you because He lives on the inside. "Endurance is not about knowing that every step you take will always be the right one but it's about moving forward even when you don't always get it right and when things don't go as planned."

— Tiaina Doughty

Contents

Proverbs 23:18, "Your future is bright and filled with a living hope that will never fade away."

2 Timothy 1:7, "For God has not given us a spirit of timidness, nor fear, nor cowardliness but the spirit of power, love, sound judgment, soundness of mind, self-control, courage, and discipline."

Romans 5:3-5, "We can rejoice, too, when we run into problems and trials, for we know that they help us develop patience and endurance. And endurance develops strength of character, and character strengthens our confident hope of salvation. And this hope will not lead to disappointment. For we know how dearly God loves us, because he has given us the Holy Spirit to fill our hearts with his love."

Day 1

Contentment

When your circumstances change and things aren't the best, remember that God's presence never changes. Put more energy into trusting that He is here with you, that even in the bad, nothing can separate you from the love of our Heavenly Father. He is still meeting your needs according to his glorious riches.

Note that sometimes Him meeting our needs means teaching us to be content in any situation and that our happiness shouldn't be based on whether things are going good but true joy is when you know God watches over you and is fighting on your behalf. Even in the unseen, when we think things aren't working for us, press on a little longer, and you will grow through whatever it is you're facing.

"I am not saying this because I am in need, for I have learned to be content whatever the circumstances. I know what it is to be in need, and I know what it is to have plenty. I have learned the secret of being content in any and every situation, whether well fed or hungry, whether I'm living in plenty or in want. I can do all this through him who gives me strength." (Philippians 4:11-13 NIV)

Being content is a divine strength from God. Being content doesn't mean you are settling for less or have given up. Being content teaches you how to speak the best, even in the worst circumstances. Being content teaches you that there is more in you, but there is a time and a season for God to birth it out of you. Even though you may have to wait a little while in a circumstance that is hard, whatever God has said concerning your life will be so.

Scripture references: Philippians 4:19, Isaiah 14:24

Day 2
Stillness

When you find yourself feeling like hope is lost, so broken down, feeling emptied out by life, people, and your circumstances. Feeling like you can't see your way out, some prayers even are unspoken, and it seems like you are on your last breath. God has been hearing you, even the things unsaid, and He knows what you need. You've been reaching out to temporary fixes, but Jesus is waiting for you to reach out to Him.

Are you at a point where you feel deep down inside that you just need healing, to be made whole, and set free from some things? Take this moment to reflect and examine what you have been at the feet of. To be at the feet of something or someone is to give your total attention to it or them.

It's so easy to focus on problems, worry, stress, things you can't control, and so much more. Jesus waits for His people to lay everything else aside and give attention to Him as the King of Kings and Lord of Lords. To be at Jesus' feet is recognizing who He is over life's problems.

It's dangerous to be in a place where you become so distracted by life's duties and responsibilities, like Martha, that you miss what Jesus wants to say to you (Luke 10:40). When you sit at Jesus' feet, His word gives you peace about the circumstances you are going through. Your stillness in God's presence reminds you of His power over situations that can pull you into a defeated place.

While in God's presence, as you become vulnerable and let Him into your heart, parts of yourself that you thought could never be made whole will change, and your atmosphere will begin to shift, causing you to have a clearer view about life.

Day 3
Value

The area in your life that has been under attack the most is where your greatest blessing is assigned. For example, if you are constantly being attacked in your mind, it's because you have so much greatness in you that the devil will do anything to play with your mind because he doesn't want you to take hold of the true you God created you to be.

Don't let the devil talk you out of your value. God is about to get ready to show Himself evident for who He really is. When the Great I AM shows up, it is FINISHED. Eyes have not seen, nor ears have not heard what God is about to do concerning you. Don't give up! Be on guard; stand firm in the faith; be courageous; be strong. You are precious in my sight and honored, and I love you.

Scripture references: 1 Corinthians 2:9, 1 Corinthians 16:13, Isaiah 43:3

Day 4

Hallelujah

There is a call to all people to praise the Lord. When you are lost for words and don't know what to say, there is one word you can hold on to. One word, but it holds much power. Hallelujah! As you go through uncertainties, your hallelujah keeps you at a place of worship rather than a place of worry. God will send His heavenly angels to fight for you and see you through to fulfill your service here on Earth.

"Are not all angels ministering spirits sent to serve those who will inherit salvation?" (Hebrews 1:14)

When you put your hallelujah in the atmosphere, it encourages you to not complain. "Do everything without complaining and arguing." The enemy will be confused as to why you are praising God in the midst of trouble. Count it all joy when you stumble into various trials. Words have power, and God honors them. Death and life are in the power of the tongue.

Scripture references: Psalms 148, Philippians 2:14, James 1:2, Proverbs 18:21

Day 5
God-Reliance

God doesn't want you to blame yourself when uncontrollable circumstances occur in your life. As humans, we have the natural tendency to want to be our own superhero. We feel good when we have the ability to handle and solve situations. You feel unworthy and view yourself as a failure when you don't succeed how you imagined.

Even at your worst, God has a better view of you, and He also has better thoughts about you than what you think about yourself. Stop beating yourself up and making yourself feel inadequate. He created us to depend on Him, even though this world makes us feel like we are supposed to be perfect and have it all together.

The greatest encounter we can have with God is in our lowest place. So if you are at your lowest place and feel like you have hit rock bottom, know that God wants to give you love that no one else can give. He wants to come into your life and let his glory be shown through your life.

God says I will not disappoint you. I know others have let you down, but I AM A DEPENDABLE GOD, says the Lord. God wants to show you great and mighty things. God wants you to know that He loves you and adores you, even the parts of you that you don't like about yourself. God said I created you uniquely, and you weren't made to fit into the standards of this world. But you are a child of MY HEAVENLY KINGDOM, says the Lord.

Scripture references: Jeremiah 31:3; Jeremiah 33:3; Jeremiah 29:11; and Genesis 1:31

Day 6

Opportunity

Your circumstances may be constantly changing, but you can hold on to God's unchanging hand. Life may be hard for you right now, but don't forget that we serve a God that everything is easy to Him, and for Him to do.

"Ah, Lord, God! Behold, You have made the heavens and the earth by Your great power and outstretched arm. There is nothing too hard for You (Jeremiah 32:17)."

God wants us to thank him for the change, even when it doesn't always feel good because it gives Him an opportunity to show that He is God, all by himself. What He opens, no one can close; and what He closes, no one can open: I know all the things you do, and I have opened a door for you that no one can close.

Continue to be faithful to God in the little things because it opens up greater opportunities for big things to come into your life. Whoever can be trusted with very little can also be trusted with much, and whoever is dishonest with very little will also be dishonest with much."

Scripture references: Luke 16:10; Revelation 3:7-8

Day 7

Gracious God

Don't let your past keep you from praying, let that be the reason you pray even more. Guilt of what you did in the past can keep you bound down. You try to live better, but you dwell on the lifestyle you once lived. You can be open with God. God has already buried our past, but we take our own shovel and dig it back up. There is nothing we can do to make God stop loving us.

You are safe with the Lord. Your mistakes don't have to be the burden that keeps you from fully opening up to God. Our Father is reaching down His hand from heaven, awaiting for us to fully rest in Him. Take comfort in knowing your life is in His hands. "Let us come boldly to the throne of our gracious God. There we will receive his mercy, and we will find grace to help us when we need it most."

Being stuck in the past causes double-mindedness, where you are not sure of anything and doubt everything, including when you are in a good space in life but can't recognize it because you are living in a place that no longer serves you. "Draw near to God, and God will draw near to you. Wash your hands, you sinners; purify your hearts, for your loyalty is divided between God and the world."

Scripture references: Romans 8:38-39; Hebrews 4:16; James 4:8

Day 8

Draw Near

Draw near to Jesus while the time is now, for tomorrow is not promised to any of us. "And that, knowing the time, that now it is high time to awake out of sleep: for now is our salvation nearer than when we believed. The night is far spent, the day is at hand: let us therefore cast off the works of darkness, and let us put on the armor of light.

Now is not the time to be unstable and easily moved. Draw near to God, who will give you fruits that will last. The enemy wants to keep us from producing godly fruit. The enemy wants to tire people out so that we will draw back in fear, anger, and bitterness, keeping you from choosing God daily.

"You did not choose me, but I chose you and appointed you so that you might go and bear fruit—fruit that will last— and so that whatever you ask in my name the Father will give you." (John 15:16 NIV)

It's dangerous when you are in a place of knowing who God is and have no excitement or reverence for Him. There is a call for all people to draw near in their hearts; it's more than just showing up physically. If our hearts are not where God is, then the work that we do in the physical world holds no weight.

When I meet God, I don't want Him to refuse me or anyone else striving towards the path of life when we think we have it right and we don't. "Every tree that does not bear good fruit is cut down and thrown into the fire. Therefore you will recognize them by their fruits. Not everyone who says to me, 'Lord, Lord,' will enter the kingdom of heaven, but the one who does the will of my Father who is in heaven. On that day many will say to me, 'Lord, Lord, did we not prophesy in your name, and cast out demons in your name, and do many mighty works in your name?' And then will I declare to them, 'I never knew you; depart from me, you workers of iniquity.'

We build our house on the rock by hearing God's word and doing what we have learned. Everyone who hears these words of mine and does them will be like a wise man who built his house on the rock.

Scripture references: Romans 13:11-12; Matthew 7:19-24

Day 9
Dependable God

Remember that God has the final word, and His words are yes and amen.

"Jesus has the last word on everything and everyone, from angels to armies. He's standing right alongside God, and what He says goes (1 Peter 3:22)."

The words of others may let you down and you may even let yourself down with negative self-talk, but God's word is dependable. Jesus rising from the dead is the final word over sickness, sin, and disease! So know today that you will live and be encouraged, knowing the battle you are facing has already been WON! Jesus has defeated the enemy of your mind that tries to bind you with strongholds of doubt and fear.

"For the weapons of our warfare are not carnal but mighty through God to the pulling down of strongholds. Casting down imaginations, and every high thing that exalteth itself against the knowledge of God, and bringing into captivity every thought to the obedience of Christ;" (2 Corinthians 10:4-5)

Day 10

Wisdom

Use wisdom with what and who you are connected to. What or who you are tied to can be the very thing or person that keeps you tied down from reaching your destiny.

Test of obedience: Will you be willing to let go of the very thing or person you thought you couldn't live without? God is a jealous God; He wants nothing or no one before Him. Who you have in your ear could be the reason why you are spiritually deaf. You can't hear God clearly when your ear is full of clutter. Unclog your ears, and close off your spirit from everyone and anybody who poses a threat to your walk with Christ.

You don't allow everyone to just come into your home or car, do you? This idea goes the same for you because your body is a temple of the Holy Spirit. You are sacred because of the Divine One who lives on the inside of you. Ask God for an understanding and discerning heart.

Also remember that when what was not so clear before becomes clear to you, try not to be discouraged. Just because you may have to cut ties with someone or something, it won't be the end of the world. It's just that there are certain places and people you have to leave behind and things you have to do alone. Just God and yourself.

Until God is ready to bring people back into your life, be patient and glean on to the Lord for His strength. You need wisdom to ensure you don't have the wrong people in a season that is supposed to be right for you. "Wisdom is the principal thing; therefore get wisdom: and with all thy getting get understanding."

Scripture references: Exodus 34:14; 1 Kings 3:9; 1 Corinthians 6:19; Proverbs 4:7

Day 11

Healing Words

God wants you, as a believer in Christ Jesus, to watch your tongue, being careful with what you speak. Your words play a part in your atmosphere shifting, and what you say holds more weight than you may realize.

"Gracious words are a honeycomb, sweet to the soul and healing to the bones (Proverbs 16:24)."

Pray over yourself that God places a guard over your mouth, it is necessary. You want good things in life, speak good things, put the word of God on everything! You will have what you say. When you speak negative words out of your mouth, you are responsible for drinking your own deadly poison. Once you release words out of your mouth, you can never take them back. Blessings and cursing come out of the same mouth. It's important to pray daily.

Prayer: Save me Lord, from lying lips and deceitful tongues and "let the words of my mouth and the meditations of my heart be pleasing in Your sight, Lord, my Rock, and my Redeemer.

Scripture references: James 3:10; Psalms 120:2; Psalms 19:14

Day 12

Grace

God has everything you need, plus more. "And God can give you more blessings than you need, and you will always have plenty of everything. You will have enough to give to every good work" (2 Corinthians 9:8). Don't be afraid to open up to God when you have days that all you can see are your weaknesses.

"My grace is sufficient for you, for my power is made perfect in weakness." (2 Corinthians 12:19)

There will be days when you need encouragement more than other days. During those days, it's important to know how to pour into yourself after constantly pouring into everyone else. Everyone has experienced being worn out or down, and if that is currently where you are, Proverbs 11:25 reads, "The generous will prosper; those who refresh others will be refreshed." When we come into God's presence, we don't have to come all "high and mighty." We don't have to pretend, like we pretend with others, that we "got it all together."

God knows about every broken part of us. He wants us to come to Him with honesty, being real about how we are feeling. God provides an atmosphere where you can put all your cards on the table without fear of being hurt. God wants you healed and whole. God is the only One who can truly fill any void we are feeling deep within.

"I will be glad and rejoice in your unfailing love, for you have seen my troubles, and you care about the anguish of my soul." (Psalms 31:7

Day 13

Endurance

There is a freshness that's coming into your life. Patience and endurance are what you need now, so that you will continue to do God's will. Then you will receive all that he has promised. Get ready for you to change. Sometimes we pray and ask God to change our circumstances, and when it doesn't seem like He hears us because we see "no change," it's easy to lose hope and feel discouraged.

God wants to change something within you; your trials and frustrations are teaching you how to keep pressing on. Press, press, press, press, press, because the shift that's happening in you will shift what's happening on the outside of you. You don't have to beat yourself up because you feel as if you haven't achieved perfection. I press on toward the goal for the prize of the upward call of God in Christ Jesus.

There is a time for everything and a season for every activity under the heavens. There is a level of insufficiency in humans that was created for us to rely on God. Our heart was created to have eternity in it. God has made everything beautiful for its own time. He has planted eternity in the human heart, but even so, people cannot see the whole scope of God's work from the beginning to end. We are all longing for a place called "Home". God doesn't want us to go astray depending on "this or that." This world trains us to recognize what's around us, worshiping what we have instead of recognizing God every day and giving thanks for who He is.

"The grass withers and flowers fade, but the word of our God stands forever." (Isaiah 40:8 NKJV)

Scripture references: Hebrews 10:36; Philippians 3:14; Ecclesiastes 3:1, 11

Day 14
Help

One Body that was broken, one Spirit that was raised, and the royal blood that was shed for humanity to live—that we would have abundant life. This is real love—not that we love God, but that He loves us and sent His Son as a sacrifice to take away our sins. Whatever your day holds, know that God is near to you. Heaven is helping you; you can breathe now.

"Let us therefore come boldly unto the throne of grace, that we may obtain mercy and find grace to help in time of need." (Hebrews 4:16)

Everything concerning your life will be beautiful in its timing. Smile and be encouraged, knowing that in the end of what you're going through, the sun is going to shine, and the rainbow is coming after the storm and rain. Pick your head up and wipe your tears; you are not forgotten.

"Why am I discouraged? Why is my heart so sad? I will put my hope in God! I will praise him again—my Savior and my God!" (Psalms 42:11)

No matter what your situation looks like or even the emotions you feel, know that God, El Roi, sees you. He knows your name and cares about your situation. We can say with confidence, "The Lord is my helper, so I will have no fear. What can mere people do to me?

Scripture references: 1 John 4:10; Genesis 16:13; Hebrews 13:6

Day 15

Purpose

God's words of encouragement for us today is for us to remember that He is an on time God and he can never fail. We all hold different purposes for where we are in life.

"For we are God's handiwork, created in Christ Jesus to do good works, which God prepared in advance for us to do" (Ephesians 2:10).

We sometimes think we are out of place or that our life is unfixable. We can become pessimistic and lose hope because of how long things are taking to change. We don't always understand God's timing and want to rush things. God is faithful and shows up to refresh us when we need it. We are all fighting hard and dark battles behind closed doors.

We all have something on the inside of us—a word of encouragement, a hug, an act of kindness, or a token of love—to help someone else, even in the midst of us needing help. What you are currently going through is attached to someone else's healing and deliverance. We just aren't healed for the sake of our own purposes, but for the purpose of others.

"To appoint unto them that mourn in Zion, to give unto them beauty for ashes, the oil of joy for mourning, the garment of praise for the spirit of heaviness; that they might be called trees of righteousness, the planting of the LORD, that he might be glorified." (Isaiah 61:3)

Prayer: Help me, Lord to be a good servant to others around me. As you are so patient, kind, and loving to me, help me to recognize the humanity in others. Help me to not be so easily offended and take things personally. Help me to engage with others like you would do. Bless me that I would be a blessing to others and not a curse. In the name of Jesus, I pray, Amen.

Day 16

Look Again

There is power in going back to look again! What "unanswered prayers" are currently blinding you and causing you to miss the answered prayers that's right in front of you. God says I'm doing that very thing for you that I promised you, but you don't perceive it yet. look again, says the Lord. I'm working it out. I am your Father in Heaven, who can never fail. I'm getting ready to come through for you again.

Keep your eyes up, and don't look down or around you. Stay focused on me, says the Lord. I'm bringing it to pass! Give God time and be patient with Him as He is patient with you. Shift out of your bad attitude and into a thankful attitude for the prayers that have already been answered. "Then Elijah said to his servant, "Go and look toward the sea." The servant went and looked. He said, "I see nothing." Elijah told him to go and look again. This happened seven times."

You may have to go back to a place where the first couple of times you didn't see anything, but go in faith and believe that if God is telling you your miracle is in a specific place, then it is so. What started off as small will increase into something greater. The seventh time, the servant said, "I see a small cloud. It's the size of a man's fist. It's coming from the sea."

Elijah told the servant, "Go to Ahab. Tell him to get his chariot ready and to go home now. If he doesn't leave now, the rain will stop him." After a short time, the sky was covered with dark clouds. The wind began to blow. Then a heavy rain began to fall.

Scripture references: 1 Kings 18:43; 1 Kings 18:44-45

Day 17

The Hills

God is your Keeper. You will not be shaken or moved because the Lord himself preserves you. God is picking you up and turning you around.

I will lift up my eyes to the hills—From whence comes my help? My help comes from the Lord, Who made heaven and earth. (Psalms 121:1-2)

The storms of life may currently have you spinning in circles. It may even seem like you are going to land flat on your face when everything is said and done. You may even feel bruised up right now, but know that God is SHIELDING you. God has a covenant which cannot be removed from His children.

"The mountains may move, and the hills disappear, but even then my faithful love for you will remain. My covenant of blessing will never be broken," says the Lord, who has mercy on you (Isaiah 54:10 NLT).

God is reminding you to trust the process. I know you are experiencing many disruptions, says the Lord, but know that those interruptions won't interfere with the "impossible" I'm doing in your life. We serve a covenant keeping God. Resist the lies of the enemy, stay steadfast in My holy word, says the Lord. I will deliver you like I promised.

Day 18
Delight

God always has you in mind. He adores you and takes delight in His children. Come as you are, says the Lord, and I will handle the rest. He is the Lord who places a new heart and spirit within us. You are not too damaged, difficult, or messed up for God. He can handle you, being that He formed you in your mother's womb.

You don't have to be afraid to pray and ask God to make His presence known to you. If you need wisdom, ask our generous God, and He will give it to you. He will not rebuke you for asking. But when you ask Him, be sure that your faith is in God alone. Do not waver, for a person with divided loyalty is as unsettled as a wave of the sea that is blown and tossed by the wind.

Sometimes we wonder where God is in the midst of what we are going through. Though unseen, the Lord is present. God has not abandoned you. You will OVERCOME. Isaiah 41:10 tells us, "So do not fear, for I am with you; do not be dismayed, for I am your God. I will strengthen you and help you; I will uphold you with my righteous right hand."

Scripture references: John 3:16; Romans 5:8; Zephaniah 3:17; Ezekiel 36:26; Jeremiah 1:5; Psalm 139:13; James 1:5-6

Day 19

Clarity

In your secret place, get ready for God to give you clarity over the confusion you've been experiencing—a spirit and mind aligned with forwardness and focus instead of backwardness and distraction. The devil seeks to devour, and he gets pleasure when you are disgruntled, and your spirit is disturbed.

More than lately, you have been battling with the spirit of unsettlement in the mind and body. You toss and turn throughout the night. Remember, the Lord is your shepherd in the valley of the shadow of death. Our troubles are just a shadow.

Jesus faced and defeated death for us whenever He took back the keys of death and hell from Satan. The shadow of death doesn't have power over us because death and hell didn't have power over Jesus! And God placed all things under his feet and appointed him to be head over everything. The Word of God is your weapon for the rest you need.

Scripture references: 1 Peter 5:8; Psalms 23:1-4; Revelation 1:8; Ephesians 1:22

Day 20
Gentleness

It's so easy to get offended and misunderstand each other. Our patience is something that gets tested DAILY. It requires patience to interact with others and deal with the demands of life. It's so easy to get caught off guard, and when you respond too quickly to a person or situation, you forget to put a check on your tongue and your attitude. Slow down and breathe. There is peace in stillness.

Prayer: Lord, when I'm being tested, bless me that I will respond back with a gentle answer. Bless me with self-control so that I will have a soothing tongue that will deescalate situations and not cause things to escalate and become worse.

You know I'm human, Heavenly Father; I often fall short. Please forgive me for all my sins, known and unknown. Give me the maturity that I won't allow my emotions to make my decisions and a spirit of love, peace, and patience so that I can endure on my journey. I'm praying that my cup will run over and overflow in Your presence.

Support me with Your unfailing love. When anxiety and worry is great within me, comfort me, Oh God. Whenever I try to do things in a hurry, working out of a hasty spirit. Teach me how to be still. Bless me to where I can truly trust in You Heavenly Father, and I would believe You will supply all my needs. Help my unbelief. In Jesus' name, I pray, Amen."

Scripture references: James 1:4; James 1:19; Proverbs 15:18; Psalms 94:17-19

Day 21

Restoration

This devotional message is focused on the readers who feel like they have been let down and need to be restored from life's hurts. You may even know someone who comes to mind when you read this, and you may even find yourself whispering a sweet prayer to heaven on their behalf.

Maybe you have someone in your life who has fallen away from what they used to know to be true and everything they once believed. Share this devotional message with someone you feel would be blessed by it.

God sees that you have lost sight and pushed Him out of your visions and plans. To lose sight of someone means there is an increased distance between the other person and yourself. You may have said a few prayers, and things didn't happen how you planned. Someone you loved may have died after you asked God to keep them here longer, the job you were hoping to get didn't come through, or the help that you wanted never arrived. The disappointment from the hurts you have experienced when you didn't have an explanation for why certain things had happened to you.

It's easy to blame God whenever your life is falling apart, and you once believed in His ability to make things better, except things seemed to be getting worse day by day. Even after all of that, there is still room for you to be restored and reconciled. You can make God first priority again in your life as He restores your soul.

Even though you have forgotten about God, know that He hasn't forgotten about you. Our Heavenly Father longs for you and is awaiting your return with open arms. God cares about your broken heart. "Turn from your fleshly ways and ask my Holy Spirit to guide you back to me."

If my people, who are called by my name, will humble themselves, pray, seek my face, and turn from their wicked ways, then I will hear from heaven, and I will forgive their sin and will heal their land. (2 Chronicles 7:14)

"You may think you separated yourself from Me, but I have been with you all along, and I will continue to be with you everywhere you go," says the Lord.

"I am with you and will watch over you wherever you go, and I will bring you back to this land. I will not leave you until I have done what I have promised you." (Genesis 28:15 NIV)

Day 22

Supply

Whenever we make a conscious decision to be people after God's heart and not just His blessings, then God sees that He can trust us and exceed all we could have ever imagined. "I have been young, and now am old; yet have I not seen the righteous forsaken, nor his seed begging bread." God would rather we correct ourselves in Him before we wreck ourselves in fleshly desires. "But if we evaluated and judged ourselves honestly [recognizing our shortcomings and correcting our behavior], we would not be judged."

Trust that He will heal your body, trust that He will regulate your mind, trust that you can walk in your authority to trample upon every enemy, and trust that whatever you need, He will supply it abundantly and give you far more than what you have hoped for.

"But for you who fear my name, the sun of righteousness shall rise with healing in its wings. You shall go out leaping like calves from the stall." (Malachi 4:2)

The type of fear we should have of God is not just being afraid of Him; to fear God is to reverence Him. Revere means to strongly admire, honor, and have high respect for something or someone.

Scripture references: Psalms 37:25; 1 Corinthians 11:31

Day 23
Establish

Even in a world where there are shortages and not enough supply for people, God knows how to set His people up with more than enough. Oftentimes, we make plans, and things don't always work out as we expect.

"Wisdom and knowledge will be the stability of your times, And the strength of salvation; The fear of the Lord is His treasure." (Isaiah 33:6)

Get ready for God's favor to rest on you. Get ready to see the manifestation of God establishing the work of your hands. May the favor of the Lord our God rest on us; establish the work of our hands for us.

God is realigning and reestablishing your heart and mind in Him. As you plant yourself to dwell in My presence, and My holy word says the Lord, I'm planting you in rooms your feet have never touched ground on. I'm increasing the might of your hands to create.

God is getting ready to make you glad for as many days as you have been afflicted. Your joy is getting ready to be doubled for all the sorrow you went through. Get ready to be satisfied by God's unfailing love.

Scripture references: Psalms 90:17; Psalm 90:15; Psalms 90:14

Day 24

Adversity

After going through so much, have you ever gotten to a point of exhaustion? Maybe you know someone who struggles with mental health and displays suicidal tendencies. Encourage them today and share this scripture with them.

"For you shall live and not die and declare the works of the Lord." (Psalms 118:17)

You are going to make it through to testify to others about God's amazing strength to bring you through those dark and tough battles. Give your burdens to the Lord, and he will take care of you. He will not permit the godly to slip and fall. When you feel the need to start over, "Great is His faithfulness; His mercies begin afresh each morning.

If you are thinking about ending it all, remember that none of us knows what tomorrow holds. It could be the very day God changes your life forever. God is lifting you up. He is your strength in the valley. When you feel like you have no hope and can't see the light, know that God is your hope and your light in the darkness. I know it seems like God is silent, but just trust that He is working behind the scenes for you. Jehovah Shalom is coming to your rescue. Hold your hands out because God is pouring out a heavy outpour of peace.

"Then Jesus said to the man, "Hold out your hand." So the man held out his hand, and it was restored!" (Mark 3:5)

Continue to whisper Jesus' sweet name as you call out, God is flowing through you. I won't let the darkness overtake you; I am the LORD GOD, who calms every storm and calls you to walk on water.

Scripture references: Psalms 55:22; Lamentations 3:23; Psalms 107:29; Matthew 14:29

Day 25
Salt and Light

Even when you feel like you're at your weakest, remember that someone is admiring you and taking note of your strength to go on and face another day. God refreshes those who refresh others. Just being you is enough to bless someone else. You may be the only person who will show someone kindness for the day. You may be the only Bible that someone will read.

Being that you are a part of the body of believers in Christ Jesus, we are called to be doers and not just hearers of the Word. How you act should reflect God's character. If you want to go deeper in this devotion, study The Beatitudes in Matthew 5:3-12.

"My Child, never forget the things I have taught you. Store my commands in your heart. If you do this, you will live many years, and your life will be satisfying (Proverbs 3:1-2 NLT).

God's word teaches you how to be salt and light. Jesus is a living example of what it means to be salt and light. Jesus is humble and obedient, and He sought to do His Father's will at all times, no matter the circumstance or opposition He had to face with the people from His hometown in Nazareth—religious leaders such as the Pharisees and Sadducees, Judas, the Romans, and Satan, just to name a few.

Even when you are doing your best to do the right thing, people will come up against you. Keep working unto the Lord.

Scripture references: Proverbs 11:25; James 1:22; Matthew 5:13-16; Colossians 3:23

Day 26

Increase

Your increase comes from God, not man. For promotion comes neither from the east nor the west nor from the south. But God is the judge: He takes one down from their position and raises another. I know others around you may be better off than you as far as connections, resources, and finances. People may have the upper hand because of certain positions that God has allowed them to be in but know that that can change at any moment, being that we can be up one day and down the next. God has the last say. He is the Author and Finisher of our faith. When God adds to your life, there is no sorrow attached to it. When God moves in your life, it produces a deeper level of praise and thankfulness. The more people look over you and push you to the side, the more God will increase you.

> *"O Lord, I have so many enemies; so many are against me; you are my glory, the one who holds my head high.... Victory comes from you, O Lord." (Psalms 3:1,3,8)*

Stay diligent in Me, says the Lord, and believe, I will do all that I have promised you. Look for an increase of peace, rest, new opportunities, and doors. An increase of downloads in your mind to create. If you know this word is for you, pray and ask God what way He is increasing you and how you can best prepare for how He chooses to increase you. Be open and think big because an increase could mean the opposite of what you're thinking. Appreciate what form your increase will come in because that area God is multiplying you in is the key that's going to majorly shift your life and shoot you in a new direction. Claim it and declare *increase is my portion.*

Scripture references: Psalms 75:6-7; Hebrews 12:2; Proverbs 10:22

Day 27

Chosen

If no one has ever spoken kindly to your identity or who you are as a person, or maybe even growing up, a caretaker didn't teach you how to positively build your self-esteem and practice walking in confidence, then it could have negatively impacted you, causing you to feel like a mistake from childhood and currently in your adult life.

God makes no mistakes. Which means you are not a mistake! Your life isn't a mistake, and the Lord puts emphasis on this, reminding you that He is serious about your life.

"And God saw everything that he had made, and behold, it was very good. And there was evening, and there was morning, the sixth day." (Genesis 1:31)

Others may downplay you, and you may even downplay yourself, but God is lifting you up. You've been feeling like a mistake all your life, and you are to the point that you want to tap out and throw in the towel. You are here because God wants you here. He created you as His son or daughter, made in His image.

"So God created man in his own image, in the image of God he created him; male and female he created them." (Genesis 1:27)

But I'm here to encourage and remind you that God has called you to live. If you tap out now and throw in the towel, you won't get the preparation you need for your promotion. God says, "I'm sending you encouragement; just be open to receive."

Let each one of us [make it a practice to] please to do what is right and to build our neighbor up spiritually in the Lord." (Romans 15:2 (AMP)

Day 28

Expectancy

Have a high expectation to see the Lord move on your behalf today and throughout this week. No matter how your morning may start, repeat these words throughout the day when you are feeling burdened: I have high hopes for my God to move mountains on my behalf, and I believe I will see what I say.

It's easy for us to be cynical because we can feel like, "I'm going back to the same job, seeing the same people." Or we are used to having a routine set for how we think our day is going to go, then a challenge pops up. Seek God always, putting Him first above all things. Speak the word over your life!

"But as for me, I will look to the Lord and be confident in Him. I will keep watch; I will wait with hope and expectancy for the God of my salvation; my God will hear me (Micah 7:7)."

No matter what this week or month throws at you, keep your expectations high. "I will listen with expectancy to what God the Lord will say, for He will speak peace to His people, to His saints those who are in right standing with Him but let them not turn again to foolish ways (Psalms 85:8)."

Prayer: Bless me this day and going forward, Lord, that even if I can't see you, I will be able to feel you ever so closely in me. Give me the courage I need to bring my requests to you, God, and I ask that Your Holy Spirit help me wait patiently with a healthy expectation of the manifestation of my prayers being sent up. Help me to see that You love this current version of myself as I'm growing to be the version of myself You called me to be. Bless me that I will never doubt Your love for me, Heavenly Father. In Jesus' name, I pray, Amen.

Day 29
Father and Friend

It's not God's plan for you to sit in silence and suffer, drowning in our pain, sorrow, setbacks, and disappointments. Reach out to someone trusted if you have that support system available. If you were once like me and had trust issues with people because of hurt, ask God to reveal and give you the discernment to know who to go to so that you all can pray together.

"Iron sharpens iron, and one man sharpens another." (Proverbs 27:17)

The enemy's plan is for our minds and hearts to get so heavy that we can't go on any longer. There are still good-hearted and genuine people out here. Don't let the devil make you believe the lie that no one cares about you. If the enemy can get you isolated, then he'll take the step forward to make sure you're annihilated to the point of no return.

Prayer: Heavenly Father, I know you're here with me. Your word tells me you'll never leave nor forsake me, but right now I'm struggling, and I need someone I can talk to and relate to in physical human form. I appreciate You being my all-in-all. You are the GREATEST friend I can have, but God, would you send me destiny helpers and remove every destiny destroyer out of my life?

I thank you in advance, God, for answering this prayer with glory speed. In the meantime, bless my spirit to be calm and lifted in You. I pray that I will be open enough to receive Your guidance, Heavenly Father, and not doubt the path that's been set for me before the hands of time. In Jesus' name I pray, Amen.

Day 30

The Holy Ghost and Fire

There are more for you and on your side than those against you. God has an army of Holy Fire to consume whatever is trying to overtake you. Don't ever let the enemy make you believe that you are OUTNUMBERED. You have an army of heavenly hosts fighting on your behalf. When God is on your side, there is no worldly enemy or spiritual enemy who can stand against our

Others may be preying on you, plotting your downfall, but remember, Jesus is praying for you to be raised up right in the presence of your enemies. Jesus lives to intercede for you (Hebrews 7:25). WHO CAN STAND AGAINST KING JESUS!

"When the servant of the man of God rose early in the morning and went out, behold, an army with horses and chariots was all around the city. And the servant said, "Alas, my master! What shall we do?" He said, "Do not be afraid, for those who are with us are more than those who are with them." Then Elisha prayed and said, "O LORD, please open his eyes so that he may see." So the LORD opened the eyes of the young man, and he saw, and behold, the mountain was full of horses and chariots of fire all around Elisha (2 Kings 6:15-17)."

Day 31
The Sheep of His Pasture

No matter how many "no's" you get or how rejected you may feel, remember God has a special place for you in this world.

"Know that the LORD is God. It is he who made us, and we are his; we are his people, the sheep of his pasture." Psalms 100:3

Don't be discouraged, get up from that discouraged place and praise God because your better is coming.

"The glory of this present house will be greater than the glory of the former house,' says the LORD Almighty. And in this place I will grant peace'..." (Haggai 2:9)

The key to success in God's eyes is in all that we do, let it be done in Jesus' name.

"I tell you the truth, anyone who believes in me will do the same works I have done, and even greater works because I am going to be with the Father." (John 14:12)

Receiving "no's" means your "yes" is right around the corner. Remain hopeful and be free, knowing what's for you will come in its timing and no one can take that away from you. Just believe and be patient!

"From the beginning I revealed the end. From long ago I told you things that had not yet happened, saying, "My plan will stand, and I'll do everything I intended to do (Isaiah 46:10)."

Day 32

Lamp Unto My Feet

Prayer: Heavenly Father, I want to go all the way with You. I have had my time in this world and given my ungodly lifestyle all of me. Now, God, I need Your Holy Spirit to do a new work on the inside of me. Bless me to lay down every weight and the sin that so easily entangles me. Help me to deny myself and take up my cross and follow You, Lord.

When I tried things my way, I was lost, going in circles and getting the same empty results. Let your word be a lamp unto my feet and a light unto my path. I need Your guidance so I can walk upright. I want to make room for you Jesus. I admit I have become accustomed to this world, and I need my mind to be renewed in you.

I thank You this day for the mercy on my life and that I get another chance to repent and make things right with You. Bless me that I just won't talk from mouth confession but let my heart match the words coming out of my mouth. Thank you for your love that covers my sins and the reason I can go forward living a faith-filled and abundant life. Thank you for redeeming me from myself and allowing me to taste and see that You are good, lord and awesome.

Scripture references: Hebrews 12:1, Matthew 16:24, Romans 12:2, Psalms 199:105

Day 33
Captured By Grace

God created each of us beautifully because we are made in His image. He is the maker of the sun, moon, and stars. If God can make the skies beautiful, believe He's making your life beautiful too. You just have to believe and be patient long enough to see all God has in store for you.

When you feel like you don't belong or have a place in this world, remember that you belong to the GREAT I AM.

He says, "I knew you long before you were even created, and I accept you! I'm capturing you, so even when you think you will fall, I won't let you fail. I know things may not be going according to your plans but believe that things are working according to My purpose for your life.

I'm teaching you to know Me and how to call out to Me through this uncomfortable circumstance. I'm watching you closely and eyeing your every step. Keep stepping and remain hopeful, before you know it this next step you're about to take will have you stepping into the miracle you've been waiting for. Be joyful in hope, patient in affliction, faithful in prayer.

Scripture references: Genesis 1:27, Exodus 3:14, Jeremiah 1:4, Romans 8:28, Romans 12:12

Day 34

Triumph

Praise be unto God because He's getting ready to cause you to triumph over every enemy! Spiritually and physically, those who wanted to see you go down, are getting ready to experience what they wished or sent to destroy you. Unless they repent and turn to God asking Him to come in their hearts and change their wicked ways.

"Let the wicked forsake his way, and the unrighteous man his thoughts; let him return to the LORD, that he may have compassion on him, and to our God, for he will abundantly pardon." (Isaiah 55:7)

We serve a merciful God, even when we do wrong, He's gracious enough to forgive us and doesn't give us the punishment we deserve.

This is the season of divine strategy. Your ears shall hear a word behind you, saying, this is the way, walk in it. Whenever you turn to the right hand or whenever you turn to the left Get ready for God to give you revelation on the plan and how He wants you to implement it! God is clearing the path and making way, the only excuse is yourself. If God is removing your enemies from around you, the only person who can stop you is YOU.

Scripture references: Psalms 27:6, Psalms 63:9, Isaiah 30:21

Day 35

Personal Growth

Sometimes it takes us to go through certain tests several times for us to see our own growth. It's easy to feel discouraged and say, "Why do I keep having to encounter these same experiences?" We may even question ourselves and believe we've got life all wrong when the truth is, we have just adjusted to viewing our own selves in a wrong manner.

When you fully understand you're not who you used to be, that's when you are really able to tap into the you, you were destined to be. You will see that you have changed when you don't respond how you used to. When you learn that in certain situations, a response is not required. You learn when to speak and when to be quiet.

Sometimes we can look at ourselves and still see the old us and miss that God has actually changed and matured us, but we don't perceive it based on the circumstances we are currently in.

We must learn to celebrate our personal growth and accomplishments, "big and small." What's small to you may be big to someone else, and what's big to you may be small for someone else. Just be kind to yourself and others. Celebrate YOU for who you are becoming and uplift others along the way.

We ask God to give you complete knowledge of His will and to give you spiritual wisdom and understanding. Then the way you live will always honor and please the Lord, and your lives will produce every kind of good fruit. All the while, you will grow as you learn to know God better and better (Colossians 1:9-10).

Day 36

Goodness of God

No matter what today brings, remember you serve the God Almighty who will always bring you through. "I will lead the blind by ways they have not known, along unfamiliar paths I will guide them; I will turn the darkness into light before them and make the rough places smooth. These are the things I will do; I will not forsake them" (Isaiah 46:16). If you are in an unknown place right now in your journey and things don't make sense, just believe God will not let the light of your heart go out.

Let all people give thanks to the Lord for His goodness, and for His wonderful works for all humanity. For He satisfies the longing soul, and fills the hungry soul with goodness. (Psalm 107:8-9)

Prayer: Lord, I thank you for the joy and peace that you've given me today. This is a new day that I can live in new mercies. I can forgive myself and others because I don't have to hold on to grudges that would only burden me.

Bless me that I won't keep replaying and rehearsing all the bad that has happened in my life but give me the courage Lord that I would only rehearse your goodness. Thank You for Your faithfulness, God bless my heart to believe that You would bring me through this trying circumstance. God bless those who are going through worse situations than I am, forgive me when I complain Lord because I know right now someone wishes that they were in my shoes right now.

It's someone who stands in need of the things that I do have, God I pray that you would bless and cover every household, give every soul around the world what they need. Give us this day our daily bread, and give us the eyes and ears we need to perceive your provision.

Oftentimes we miss whenever you are speaking to us because we have put you in a box. Strengthen me Heavenly Father that I would take the limits off of you. I thank you for the blood of Jesus that washes me and covers me thru and thru. In Jesus' sweet name I pray, Amen.

Day 37

Living for God

God is honoring your effort. God sees the desire you have to honor Him by striving to do what is right. He sees your faithfulness through trials. You are not perfect, and God knows that, but Our Heavenly Father sees your faithfulness. He knows your heart and how you want to do His will above everything else. In pursuing God's will comes wisdom. Your labor hasn't been in vain.

The Lord says, "I will rescue those who love me. I will protect those who trust in my name.... I will reward them with a long life and give them my salvation." The answer you are looking for will come as you continue to journey on. "I know the going gets tough but stay consistent and persistent in Me," says the Lord.

Continue to show yourself trustworthy with the "little" you have been given and watch God multiply your "little" to something much BIGGER than you can imagine. God wants His children to be confident in knowing that He has our back, and we can do what He's called us to do through His might, power, Spirit, and strength!

By His divine power, God has given us everything we need for living a godly life. We have received all of this by coming to know Him, the one who called us to himself by means of his marvelous glory and excellence. And because of His glory and excellence, He has given us great and precious promises. These are the promises that enable you to share His divine nature and escape the world's corruption caused by human desires."

Scripture references: Psalms 91:14,16, 2 Peter 1:3-4

Prayer according to Psalms 143:10: Heavenly Father, teach me to do Your will daily, for You are my God; Your Spirit is good. Lead me in the land of uprightness. In Jesus name, Amen.

Day 38
Power of God

This is a season where God is encouraging and nudging His children to face every fear. The supernatural strength you need will come from the Power of God. God is calling us out to do those things that we fear the most. For God has not given us a spirit of fear, but of power and of love and of a sound mind.

What move or gift has God instructed you to start but you still remain seated on what you have been called to walk in?

"Do not be afraid of them or their hostile faces, For I am with you always to protect you and deliver you," says the LORD." (Jeremiah 1:8)

God is easing your anxious mind starting today! The Lord has granted you access and success! As you get in God's presence and continue to seek Him expect to see a change! "My grace is all you need. My power works best in weakness. What was once standing in your way will fall."

"What then are we to say about these things? If God is for us, who is against us? He who did not withhold his own Son, but gave him up for all of us, will he not with him also give us everything else? Who will bring any charge against God's elect? It is God who justifies (Romans 8:31-33)."

Scripture references: 2 Timothy 1:7; 2 Corinthians 12:9

Day 39

Pray for One Another

Sometimes the one who is always causing the problems won't see a problem at all. We can't force anyone to understand what they don't see as an issue. We have to pray for one another when we see each other falling short instead of gossiping and talking behind each other's backs. God doesn't allow us to see things to judge one another, but to pray in a spirit of love for God to save and fix whatever is wrong within the person, which will bring forth healing.

"Therefore confess your sins to each other and pray for each other so that you may be healed. The prayer of a righteous person is powerful and effective (James 5:16).

A responsibility of a seer is to view others from God's eyes, praying according to the Spirit and not just what we are seeing carnally and from a fleshy place. When God summons and calls you, He chooses what gifts to bless you with. We have to pray for discernment and maturity to handle what God has given us.

Prayer: Lord, teach me how to be as wise as a serpent and as innocent as a dove, help me to do what I'm supposed to do with what you've given me. Thank you for giving me the wisdom, sight, and hearing that I won't be ignorant of Satan's devices and schemes When enemies seek to destroy me God, I praise you for being my protection in the battlefield. You've given me life Lord, help me to stay in alignment with the abundant life you supply, and out of harm and deaths' way. In Jesus name I pray, Amen.

Scripture references: Matthew 10:7, 2 Corinthians 2:11

Day 40
Reflection

The answer we are looking for is already within us. The truth is... We are just one mindset shift, one decision away from the change we're looking for. We just don't get results based on what we say but it's WHAT WE DO!

"As a face is reflected in water, so a person is reflected by his heart." (Proverbs 27:19)

We can talk all day long but if our actions don't align with our words then it all leads down to nothing. But prove yourselves doers of the word, and not merely hearers who delude themselves. For if anyone is a hearer of the word and not a doer, he is like a man who looks at his natural face in a mirror; for once he has looked at himself and gone away, he has immediately forgotten what kind of person he was.

Prayer: Lord, break every bad habit that hinders my growth mentally, physically, and spiritually. I know I'm not a bad person, Lord, but my habits don't always help me reach the goals I set. The comfort of familiarity sometimes holds me back. Jesus, I need your strength to overcome. Help me to see myself stronger so that I won't keep operating out of the weak place I see myself in. I know better, Lord, but I need the discipline and self-control to do better. I need your Spirit to empower me to break every bad habit so that I can walk in divine alignment with the plan You have for my life. In Jesus name, I pray, Amen.

Scripture references: James 1:22-24

Day 41

Redirection

YOU ARE GOING TO MAKE IT! I want you to know there is another way. I know the way you thought you were going to take to get to your destination didn't work out or go as planned but God REROUTED YOU FOR A REASON.

"A man's heart plans his way, But the LORD directs his steps."
(Proverbs 16:9)

When God reroutes you it doesn't mean you won't get to where you're going, it just means he has a better way. Don't lose hope, keep your heart lifted in the Lord because Jesus is the way, the truth, and the life (John 14:6). Thank God for Him rerouting you because it saved your life from what could have killed you spiritually and physically.

Prayer: Lord, I thank You for seeing the dangers that I don't see. I praise You for saving me from the seen and unseen. Keep my heart and mind Steadfast in you and your faithfulness Lord. In Jesus name I pray. Amen.

Day 42

Preserve

Others may have seen your struggle and overlooked you. But God is sending you help to lighten your load. God has heard your every prayer, 1 John 5:14 tells us, *"This is the confidence we have in approaching God: that if we ask anything according to his will, he hears us."*

He has also captured each of your tears in a bottle, when you didn't have the words to speak out in prayer. The people God is sending to you are praying on the right way on how to help you versus the people who have preyed on you for the wrong ways to hurt you.

God has His eyes on you. Right now someone is observing your life looking for a way they can bless you. God has granted you favor with man and wants me to remind you that He favors you in spite of your enemies.

"You have granted me life and favor, And Your care has preserved my spirit." (Job 10:12)

Let's praise and thank God in advance for the help, from taking us from struggling and humiliated to prosperous and successful. Let's get personal with God because He knows your name.

Scripture references: Psalms 56:8, Exodus 33:17

Day 43

Bloom

God cares about your life's journey. He cares about the storms in your life and even the heavy rain. God wants us to remember to bloom and flourish where we are planted!

"Blessed is the man who trusts in the LORD, and whose hope is the LORD. For he shall be like a tree planted by the waters, which spreads out its roots by the river, and will not fear when heat comes; but its leaf will be green, and will not be anxious in the year of drought, nor will cease from yielding fruit." (Jeremiah 17:7-8)

That feeling of inadequacy you've had following you your whole life, feeling like you're not good enough. Every part of you that feels insufficient from the inside to the out, the king of kings is your sufficiency.

If you're lacking love, you got it with Jesus. If you're lacking peace, you've got it in Jesus. If you are in need of healing physically, spiritually, mentally, or emotionally, you've got it with Jesus.

Jesus bore everything about you on the cross from low self-esteem, identity confusion, sickness, addiction, and whatever else it is that you are currently facing! You name it, Jesus covered it! Jesus died and rose again on the third day so that you can be free to live in His grace and mercy.

The Lord is not slack at keeping His promises. Hold on to the promises of the Most High. Keep lifting His name up and believing. Your life is an example, a living witness of what God can do! None of us have "arrived" yet. We won't be complete until the day of Christ's return. Wait with the expectation of the glory of God to be revealed through your life. What God can and will do in your life is worth the wait. The other side of where you are currently is much sweeter, if you just hold on a little longer.

Day 44
God's Ability

"¹² But the Lord made the earth by his power, and he preserves it by his wisdom. With his own understanding he stretched out the heavens. ¹³ When he speaks in the thunder, the heavens roar with rain. He causes the clouds to rise over the earth. He sends the lightning with the rain and releases the wind from his storehouses." (Jeremiah 10:12-13 NLT)

God is meeting you right where you are! Whatever it is that you're facing, you are going to get through it by God's ability. Sometimes it's easy to look at ourselves and feel discouraged because we know that our ability is limited. When God calls you to a thing, He's the one who will bring you through it.

Keep your head lifted and looking up to Jesus. When you walk in God's ability, he'll never let you fail because His name is attached to all that you do.

"So whether you eat or drink or whatever you do, do it all for the glory of God." (1 Corinthians 10:31)

Prayer: Lord, bless me to be led by your Spirit at all times. Let every decision I make from here on out be led by your Spirit. Help me to walk by the Spirit, talk by the Spirit, see by the Spirit, and hear by the Spirit. Give me the strength in You to keep my mind and body and bring it to full submission to the life you have called me to live according to your word Lord. In Jesus name I pray, Amen.

Day 45

Clothed in Grace

There is glory attached to your story. The tougher your story, the greater God's glory. What you are going through is part of your testimony that will show off the evidence of how God brought you through. To reign with Christ is to suffer with Christ. I know that some things we go through in life make us feel as if we didn't deserve it.

But we have to remember that Jesus paid and died a criminal's death on a cross, yet He knew no sin. Right now you may be in a place where you feel like you are at a point of no return, but I declare and decree, as we touch and agree that the Holy Spirit will bring you back and place you on solid ground.

God is pulling you through, don't get stuck where you are! You won't be found in that pit of darkness any longer, you will rise to be found in the foundation of who God is! Make yourself available to God just like how you make yourself available to everything and everybody else and watch how God turns things around. How you spend our time matters.

Where God has placed you He will grace you, even if the circumstance seems unimaginable. God will clothe you in His grace, no matter what it is you have to face!

Scripture references: 2 Timothy 2:12, Philippians 2:8,

Day 46

Peace and Harmony

Prayer For Today:

Lord, Bless me to see the positive in everything. I bind up the spirit of negativity right now. No longer will a negative spirit hinder my daily life. Break every bond of toxic thinking and toxic cycles with Your consuming Holy Fire.

Take up every empty space in me, Lord. Fill my temple up with Your presence. The devil wants me to meditate on that one offense, that one situation or circumstance, and for me to not see the good that's still in my midst. The enemy will do anything to cause me to miss my blessings. But this morning, I am praying for God's strength to see me through.

God, I ask that You help me to turn my attention to You only, and not to negativity. Heavenly Father, help me to live a devoted life to You. I need the power of Your Holy Spirit to renew my mind, change the way I think, and live in peace and harmony with those around me. No matter what's going on in my life, let it always be fresh praise for You Lord, coming from the deepest part of my soul. No matter what's going on, Lord, let me be strong enough to never allow anything to take away my praise. When I am feeling the pressures of life, help me to be empowered by the power of praise. In Jesus name, I pray, Amen.

Day 47

Jesus is Matchless

Remember to keep God first in your life. It's easy to worship creation but there is only one true king. No other "god" has the power to do what the God Almighty can. No other being or thing can match the sovereignty of who God is! "Every knee shall bow in heaven, and on earth and under the earth, and every tongue shall confess that Jesus Christ is Lord." (Philippians 2:10-11)

Prayer: God, bless me that I would speak victory during my tests. No matter how real my pain feels, may Your sweet Spirit always remind me that my Redeemer lives. In a world that is unbelieving, keep me strengthened that You, Jesus would be the only One I believe in. When other gods would want to take Your place, keep me focused to build an altar daily placing You above everything. In Jesus name I pray, Amen.

Day 48
Smile

The devotion for today is simple but a life changing message! Smile, that's it, that is the message! Smile because happiness looks good on you, Smile because God has gifted you with a smile that can brighten anyone's day. A smile is one of our greatest physical traits that speaks a million words. I challenge you this day to go out of your way to make someone smile. And remember, when all else fails and you feel like you don't have a reason to smile, keep in mind that God has smiled on you this morning when he woke you up and decided you will live today!

"The LORD bless you and keep you; the LORD make his face shine upon you and be gracious to you; the LORD turn his face toward you and give you peace." (Numbers 6:25-27)

Day 49

Go in Peace

God has made us to take charge over everything concerning our life. Luke 10:19 says, "Behold, I have given you authority to tread on serpents and scorpions, and over all the power of the enemy, and nothing shall hurt you."

God doesn't call us to be powerless to spiritual forces working against our life but to raise up with power because of the name we're coming in, which is Jesus name. A reminder for God's people that God not only goes before us, but he goes before our enemies too! God is always ahead of every enemy the evil one would try to send into our lives. No matter who or what you're up against, they cannot stand against the king.

Go about your day in peace. Lay down the things that are too heavy for you and out of your control. There is a place of trust that God wants you to be led into.

"Go in peace; your way in which you are going has the Lord's approval." (Judges 18:6)

You have God's approval when you choose to trust in God as your living hope, who makes a way out of no way.

Prayer: Thank you Lord that even if the battles of life are present I can be confident in my faith that miracles are still in motion and the table is set. I can never forget your mercy and grace. My enemies can summon whoever to try to curse me but in the end I will be blessed because Your word in Exodus 14:14 tells me, *"The Lord will fight for me, and I shall* *go in peace."* I am touching and agreeing with Your word that every good work in me will be completed. Fear would only bring doubt trying to convince me that God can't bring me through, but the devil is a liar.

Philippians 1:6 speaks completion and lets us know God is able. Being confident of this, that he who began a good work in you will carry it on to completion until the day of Jesus Christ. I can be confident that I will win because I serve the God who can never lose! In Jesus mighty name I pray, Amen.

Day 50

Lessons Before Blessings

Thank God for the lessons that come before the blessings. Without the lessons you wouldn't know how to carefully manage the blessings.

"Let the wise hear and increase in learning, and the one who understands obtain guidance." (Proverbs 1:5)
"But grow in the grace and knowledge of our Lord and Savior Jesus Christ. To him be glory both now and forever! Amen." (2 Peter 3:18)

God makes no mistakes. Wisdom comes as you endure. We have to adapt the mindset of "this won't take me out because God is bringing me to an expected end." What's meant to help you will hurt you if you don't have the right mindset about it.

There is a renewal in the spirit of your mind that needs to take place daily. What you are going through is only preparing you for where God is taking you.

"Like newborn babies, crave pure spiritual milk, so that by it you may grow up in your salvation, now that you have tasted that the Lord is good." (1 Peter 2:2-3)

"When I was a child, I spoke as a child, I understood as a child, I thought as a child; But when I grew up, I put away childish things." (1 Corinthians 13:11)

Scripture references: Jeremiah 29:11, Ephesians 4:23,

Day 51

Work In Progress

In case no one has ever told you or maybe you haven't considered this about yourself, but you add value everywhere you go. There is something special on the inside of you that positively impacts those around you.

You may be feeling the demands and pressures of your responsibilities but great job with keeping your cool lately. It's easy to lash out in frustration and anger but God sees how you have been doing your best to not allow your emotions to get the best of you. With all of the "overwhelming" to-do's, you keep on pushing through.

Whatever it is you didn't get done yet, you can still be proud of what you have accomplished. You are not a failure, you are human. Which means you are a work in progress. Any goals you didn't reach for the week, don't sweat it. It's so easy to talk ourselves out of something because of fear and doubt but I want to encourage you today with a simple reminder, just keep going! You will get to where you need to be at the right time, just thank Jesus for seeing you through!

"Don't become so well-adjusted to your culture that you fit into it without even thinking. Instead, fix your attention on God. You'll be changed from the inside out. Readily recognize what he wants from you, and quickly respond to it. Unlike the culture around you, always dragging you down to its level of immaturity, God brings the best out of you, develops well-formed maturity in you." (Romans 12:2 MSG)

Day 52
Faithful Through the Generations

There is an enemy on the loose. The devil is seeking to devour you and me. The devil comes to kill, steal, and destroy. This devotion is focused on prayer to come into agreement that you shall live and not die. God has not come to play, and He needs His children to be bold and ready, in and out of season! This is an hour to be led by the Holy Spirit into fasting and praying because the enemy wants us blinded and for us not to hear or see clearly.

Prayer: Heavenly Father, Thank You for life, breath, and strength this morning. Thank You for the new mercies for today and your faithfulness throughout the ages and generations.

Thank You for being the God who is able to do exceedingly and abundantly above all we can ask, think, or imagine. Thank you for dismantling every wicked and evil plot, plan, or scheme sent by the evil one to destroy my life. Shut every evil eye, ear, and mouth that would monitor and lurk to keep ungodly tabs on me. Jesus, I thank you for the anointing and consecration that would loose the bands of wickedness, lightening the burdens of those who work for You, Lord.

Untie the cords of every ungodly yoke, set the oppressed free, and remove the chains that bind people. Every spell, every curse, every stronghold, and every root burn and die by Holy Fire. Expose every witch, warlock, and demon seeking to cause frustration in my life, spiritually manipulating my destiny, causing war against my mind and pain in my body, I make a demand on my rights, in the name of Jesus, Satan that you have no more dominion over anything concerning me.

I am taking what belongs to me by force, everything that belongs to me by the power of God's word and the name of Jesus. I declare and decree that the Glorious Realm from Heaven is opening up, destroying every hidden enemy, and shutting every demonic door and portal out of my life. I come into agreement with the power of the blood of the lamb that covers my doorpost spiritually and physically that protects me from every evil thing.

Jesus, I praise you for being my guard and shield, Who keeps me safe as I set foot out my front door today and get into my car, granting me traveling mercies, that I am safe and protected. I am free of fear, because You go ahead of me Lord and according to Your word in Psalm 91:11, I don't have to worry because You have commanded heavenly angels concerning me to guard me in all my ways, and to be by my side at all times.

Nudge my spirit Lord when I'm not supposed to go to certain places or be around certain people. I don't want to be at the wrong place at the wrong time. Every person that would want to misguide me or lead me down a deadly path, Lord I'm asking that You raise up a standard. I thank You for saving me and washing me with your blood.

I pray against freak accidents and untimely death right now in the mighty name of Jesus. That what you have not planted on the inside of me will be uprooted right now and everything that has been assigned to my life to kill, steal, or destroy me will be smashed to pieces in the mighty name of Jesus. Thank you Lord for allowing me to rest in Your Bosom. Hide me under the shadow of your wings, Lord.

I pray for my loved ones and entrust them in your hands, Lord. Guard them from evil and supply their every need according to your will. Comfort those in jail, prison, the nursing homes, overseas, those serving the country. I pray for the sick, I pray for the lost and addicted that like the prodigal son they would all be restored in you. Lead us back home to you Lord before it's too late, I know time is winding up and the devil time is almost up. Those who can be saved, do it for them, Lord.

Forgive us from everything we don't know, and all that we do know. Help us all come into and remain in good standing with you Lord. This is the prayer of your servant Lord, not perfect but a willing vessel. Help me to be an example for the lost and to encourage my brothers and sisters in Christ. In Jesus sweet name I pray, Amen.

Scripture references: 1 Peter 5:8, John 10:10, Psalms 118:17, 2 Timothy 4:2, Psalms 119:90, Ephesians 3:20

Day 53
Full Life

God has placed an angel by your side to guard you in all your ways (Psalms 91:11). No matter what you are going through, expect help from Heaven! God will open the necessary doors to get you where he has designed for you to be in this season of your life.

"I will always show you where to go. I'll give you a full life in the emptiest of places - firm muscles, strong bones. You'll be like a well-watered garden, a gurgling spring that never runs dry." (Isaiah 58:11 MSG)

Prayer: God, I'm asking You to arrest those things in my life that don't align with Your Will for me. Shut every door physically and spiritually that is meant to distract me, causing any delay and stagnation. Help me to be joyful in the midst of adversity. When I'm facing the impossible, help me to have faith, even if it is the size of a mustard seed that You Lord will and can make all things possible.

Help me to be patient and wait on Your timing Lord. Help me not to be negative but to expect nothing but the best from You Lord. When I'm feeling weary and like I can't stand any longer, lift me up Lord. When I'm feeling low, lead me to The Rock that's higher than me.

Thank You Lord for all the wonderful blessings on this day! I appreciate the breath in my lungs and that I'm not in the hospital on a breathing machine. Thank you that I can see and hear. Thank you for having food to eat and a car to drive with gas in the tank. I'm grateful for a healthy body that allows me to get up, move around and go to work. I may have a few pains and aches, but Lord You always bring me through. You are a wonderful provider, Lord. In Jesus name I pray, Amen.

Day 54

New Creation

God has the power to truly change lives! 2 Corinthians 5:17, "Therefore if anyone is in Christ, he is a new creation. The old has passed away. Behold, the new has come!" Our circumstances may change but God always remains the same. Others may not think you are worth saving, but God says otherwise.

Just when others think you're done and your time is up, God steps in and says no, her life/ his life has just begun. God says we are worth it. It's not about what we think we don't or do deserve, God is good and it's by Jesus sacrificial death and His rising through the power of the Holy Spirit that we get another chance at life.

Meditate on the times God came through for you when you didn't deserve it. There is a song with these lyrics that speaks to every believer in Christ Jesus! "You thought I was worth saving, so you came and changed my life. You thought I was worth keeping, so you cleaned me up inside. You thought I was to die for, so you sacrificed Your life. So I can be free, so I can be whole, so I can tell everyone I know!"

Even in our rebirth when we become saved we will still have troubles. We are going to experience some suffering in this life. Scripture tells us: Many are the afflictions of the righteous, but the Lord delivers them out of them all (Psalms 34:19).

Day 55

God's Care

When you're thankful you realize you have more. Being unthankful takes away from the spirit of gratitude and it makes you feel like you have less and never satisfied, always in need of something. Comparison is the thief of joy. If you're always looking at what you don't have and who you don't have in your corner, it can make you feel like you never have enough. You may not be where we want to be in life but it's time that we all start being grateful for where we are.

There is a quote that says, "I felt sorry for myself because I had no shoes, until I met a man who had no feet." Smile, show love and kindness to those you interact with daily, and be glad anyway. This is not to disregard how we feel because I know life can get hard but being negative isn't going to help our case either when we are going through life. All things will work together in its timing.

"Does worry add anything to your life? Can it add one more year, or even one day? So if worrying adds nothing, but actually subtracts from your life, why would you worry about God's care of you?" (Luke 12:25-26 TPT)

Day 56
Covered by God

God has you covered in all areas of your life. We all go through trouble and experience some hard days, but God will always see us through and stick by our side (Proverbs 18:24). What greater friend do we know or have like King Jesus, when we're going through life's challenges?

"He shall cover thee with his feathers, and under his wings shalt thou trust: his truth shall be thy shield and buckler."
(Psalms 91:4)

Prayer: Heavenly Father, I thank You for being the God over my life who arms me with strength and keeps my way secure (Proverbs 18:32). Thank You for Your Holy Spirit that fills me with Your glory and love. Help me to endure when I'm facing trials so that my faith would be genuine (1 Peter 1:7). When I'm being tested as fire tests and purifies gold, keep my heart singing praises unto You Lord. Help me to look forward to the joy ahead, but presently rejoice at how You are moving in my life right now. Life can feel lonely, but I thank You that I'm never alone because Your Holy Spirit is inside of me. In Jesus sweet name, I pray, Amen.

Day 57

Follow Jesus

This devotion is to encourage you as you make the daily choice to follow Jesus. God chooses to manifest himself to us in many ways, we just have to be open to allowing the Lord to move. No matter the circumstance, whether you are facing sickness or in good health, experiencing loss, debt, in need of financial help, or doing the best you ever have in your life. We have to make a commitment to follow God when we are in the lowest place of our life, when things aren't going well.

God is still good! When things are going well and your life is overflowing with materialistic blessings, God is still good! Our circumstances may change but God never does. The Lord knows who to send and when to send the right people in your life at the right time. We are called to be the light everywhere we go.

When following the Word of the Lord we can never go wrong. In our past life and living in deadly sins, it felt "good" like everything was going right but I'm here to encourage someone to let you know you made the right choice by devoting your life to Jesus, God sees you and knows your heart towards Him. Don't go back and give into old weaknesses, things God has delivered you from.

"And calling the crowd to him with his disciples, he said to them, "If anyone would come after me, let him deny himself and take up his cross and follow me. For whoever would save his life will lose it, but whoever loses his life for my sake and the gospel's will save it. For what does it profit a man to gain the whole world and forfeit his soul? For what can a man give in return for his soul?" (Matthew 8:34-37 ESV)

Prayer: Heavenly Father, I pray for You to strengthen my heart and mind that I won't go back to the way things used to be. Bless me to follow you Lord, no matter how hard life gets. Light up every dark place surrounding me and help my eyes to see the hope my faith in You brings to me. Every time the enemy whispers to me I'm wasting my time serving the Lord, God I thank You for elevating me and taking me higher in Your presence. Thank You Jesus for being my shield and fortress when the enemy seeks to devour me. In Jesus name I pray, Amen.

Day 58

Begin Afresh

"The faithful love of the Lord never ends! His mercies never cease. Great is his faithfulness; his mercies begin afresh each morning. I say to myself, "The Lord is my inheritance; therefore, I will hope in him!"
(Lamentations 3:22-24 NLT)

With all that God has brought you through, I'm sure you can attest and recall plenty of times that God has always shown up as faithful. There hasn't been a time where I personally ever been able to recall God not being there for me. I thank God for not always giving me what I want but what I need. His timing is perfect! In this life we won't get things how we want them, but we can still praise God for grace, mercy, love, forgiveness, and faithfulness.

"It does not, therefore, depend on human desire or effort, but on God's mercy." (Romans 9:16)

Prayer: Heavenly Father I simply want to say Thank You, for having mercy and compassion on me. Thank you for your covenant of peace and everlasting love that can never be removed from me. Thank you for being the Lord Almighty. I appreciate you for being the greatest living king and for that I can never be defeated. The devil is a liar because every victory belongs to Jesus. Thank you God for raising me up out of the deadly path I was once walking on and raising me up to live a life that glorifies the Kingdom of Heaven. In Jesus name, Amen.

Scripture references: Isaiah 54:10

Day 59
Stand Firm

There comes a point in our journey where we just have to learn to stand firm and let God's word be the only thing we choose to accept. The declaration for the day is no matter what the devil may try to do to attack my health or mind, I will accept God's word. I will not stop blessing the name of the LORD until God himself calls me home, and even then, I have the opportunity to worship Him freely with nothing holding me back.

For God, I live, and for God, I die. Every sickness has to bow to the name of Jesus. God I choose to believe you no matter what. I am a chosen people, I am a royal priesthood, a holy nation, and God's special possession.

Devil you will take your filthy hands off of everything concerning me and my life. My name spells victory! I will not be shaken, and I will not be moved. I am who God says I am. I am healed, I am whole, I am clothed in His strength and righteousness, and I am delivered and set free. No matter the attack, I won't turn against the One and true living God. I am God's chosen vessel, and I will continue to encourage and speak what God tells me to say to His people. Devil, you can't have my increase! I've been ordained and qualified by the Lord himself. I am fearfully and wonderfully made. Everything concerning my life that God has spoken over me will come to pass. The weapons may form, but they shall not prosper. God's plan will prevail through the fire and storm.

Scripture references: Romans 14:8, 1 Peter 2:9, Psalms 139:14, Deuteronomy 28:1-14

Day 60

Joy Unspeakable

In life we become discouraged every now and then. What comes to mind when you think about what steals your joy? The things that weigh heavy on you and take away from your peace of mind. Things may be unclear right now, but you will have joy again.

"Let me make it quite clear: You will weep and be over-come with grief over what happens to me. The unbeliev-ing world will be happy, while you will be filled with sor-row. But know this, your sadness will turn into joy when you see me again!" (John 16:20 TPT)

The sun will shine again in your life, those gloomy days will be filled with joy, the stormy clouds will part, and you've got a reason to live! Each of us are traveling on a path to where things are unknown, and we are waiting on answers to life's problems. In the meantime, we have to make a declaration, "I won't be afraid of the darkness because I know the One who forms light and creates darkness.

I'm no longer a slave to fear, I am a child of God. God splits the seas of my circumstances so I can walk right through it. My fears are drowned in perfect love. Though you have not seen Him, you love Him; and even though you do not see Him now, you believe in Him, and you rejoice with joy unspeakable and full of glory, for you are receiving the end result of your faith, the salvation of your souls.

Prayer: Heavenly Father, help me to fully surrender those things to you that I allow to steal my joy and take away my peace. God I pray that you would grant me my joy back and teach me to stay grounded in your peace. In Jesus name I pray, Amen.

Scripture references: 1 John 4:18, 1 Peter 8-9, Exodus 14:19-31, Isaiah 45:7

Day 61
Father of Heavenly Lights

If you are someone battling anxiety and intrusive thoughts. I know the walls of your mind feels like it will be a forever battle but believe that anxiety, depression, and worry will no longer have dominion over you. God's light overpowers any darkness.

"But when the set time had fully come, God sent his Son, born of a woman, born under the law, to redeem those under the law, so that we might receive adoption to sonship. Because you are His sons, God sent the Spirit of his Son into our hearts, the Spirit who calls out, "Abba, Father." So you are no longer a slave, but God's child; and since you are his child, God has made you also an heir." James 1:17, "Every good and perfect gift is from above, coming down from the Father of the heavenly lights, who does not change like shifting shadows." (Galatians 4:4-7)

Day 62
Possess the Land

"Behold, I have set the land before you. Enter and possess the land that the LORD swore He would give to your fathers Abraham, Isaac, and Jacob, and to their seed after them." (Deuteronomy 1:8)

Sometimes God has to remove the wrong people before He places you in the right position. We have to adapt to the mindset of "It's nothing for my God to move on my behalf." There are lessons and ways God wants to strengthen us before he moves us. God cares about the capacity of what you're ordained to carry over the comfortability of what you're experiencing.

Your comfortability can limit your capacity. Because we think we can only handle a little bit, but God sees us handling the impossible through his might, strength, infinite wisdom and power. So whatever your battle is on today, believe that God will strengthen you to reach your highest capacity.

This word capacity goes hand in hand with potential. The potency of the attack on your life only speaks for the potential God is bringing you to. God is fulfilling our potential through our hardships. The breaking has to come forth before the fulfillment. What's currently "breaking" you is actually filling you for the position.

Day 63

Forgive Others

The Lord won't fully remove your enemies out of your life because they have to watch you be blessed. People have seen your suffering and laughed, now it's time for them to see your blessings and they will be wishing they never did you how they did. Even when the enemy comes back crying, you are not obligated to accept them back in your life when God has delivered you and removed them out of your inner courts. You are obligated to forgive them because the Word of God tells us in Matthew 6:14, that if we want forgiveness from God we ourselves have to forgive others. Don't let unforgiveness keep you from your blessings.

Prayer: According to Psalms 103:12 Heavenly Father, Thank You for your forgiveness towards me, bless me to be courageous enough to forgive others when they have wronged me. In the name of Jesus I pray, Amen.

Day 64
God Of The Impossible

While facing the impossible, here are some encouraging declaration scriptures to help add to your measure of faith:

"But Jesus looked at them and said, "With man this is impossible, but with God all things are possible." (Matthew 19:26)

"Ah, Sovereign LORD, you have made the heavens and the earth by your great power and outstretched arm. Nothing is too hard for you." (Jeremiah 32:17)

God can do all things, His plans cannot be thwarted (Job 42:2)

"Know therefore today, and take it to your heart, that the Lord, He is God in heaven above and on the earth below; there is no other." (Deuteronomy 4:39)

"Pay attention, O Jacob, for you are my servant, O Israel. I, the Lord, made you, and I will not forget you. (Isaiah 44:21 NLT)

The Lord God is my strength; He will make my feet like deer's feet, and He will make me walk on my high hills. (Habakkuk 3:19)

Blessed are you who believe, for there will be a fulfillment of those things which were told to you from the Lord!" (Luke 1:45)

It will be done according to your faith (Matthew 9:29).

Be encouraged. When you cry out to God, He will answer you and He will make you bold with strength in your soul. Many people have had to experience more pain, but God just calls for faith the size of a mustard seed. God's timing is always perfect, and He Hasn't Forgotten You!

Prayer: Heavenly Father, Thank you for your unfailing love for me and your perfect plan for my life. Give me the courage to believe again, and the boldness to have unwavering faith even when it looks like things won't get better. Deepen my trust in You and strengthen me in every area I am weak. In Jesus name I pray, Amen.

Scripture references: Matthew 17:20, Psalms 138:3

Day 65
Longevity Of Life

The devotion for today's words of encouragement is about shifting your focus! When you want to worry, replace those thoughts with uplifting thoughts. The Devil wants you to look at your long list of sins and shortcomings to convince you that you are unworthy and a disgrace to God. But God wants you to look at the longevity of the dimensions and depths of grace and mercy over your life! When the Devil comes in to question your identity let him know today that I am free and forgiven!

Your past does not have ownership over you, this is a new day to walk in new mercies! God has still been faithful to each of us in spite of all that we've ever done. You can take off your boxing gloves with God, He desires to build you for His Holy Kingdom. We are declaring today that our latter days will be greater than our former days and we will have peace in every area of our life.

Prayer: Heavenly Father, help me to open up my heart and mind to You. Any area that I try to close off from You, give me the humility to let down my walls so that the King of Glory can come in and fill every part of my temple. Do a new work in my mind, heart, body, and soul for Your glory God. Help me to see myself how you see me Abba, so that I can come into alignment with the word You have purposed and set over my life. Every spirit of confusion and anxiety, I command you to flee by the authority of the Blood of Jesus! Heavenly Father, I submit my all to You this day. Give me the courage to walk in the light boldly, no longer stumbling in darkness. In Jesus name I pray, Amen.

Scripture references: Psalms 23:6, Lamentations 3:23, Psalms 91:16, Haggai 2:9)

Day 66
Substance Of Things Hoped For

The devotion for this message is to encourage you that you're getting ready to walk in new victories. I am believing with you for a life-changing shift and new beginnings. In the name of Jesus, I am believing for all new everything concerning your life! A renewal in your health, mind, finances, job, relationships, connections, and everything concerning you. You may look at your life and see no evidence, but your belief in Jesus is the evidence. Your faith is the evidence that better is on the way. As a matter of fact, better is already here!

Now faith is the substance of things hoped for, the evidence of things not seen (Hebrews 11:1)

Prayer: Heavenly Father, I'm coming to You humbly as I know how. I'm calling forth new beginnings in me, Lord. I need Your grace to help me shift from the old, the things that's not beneficial to where my new is taking me. Help me to hold on and not allow frustration to take over. Purify my attitude, Lord, and remove every temper and emotion that poses as a stumbling block in my path. I know this journey is a process, and things aren't always going to come as fast as I like. Abba, no matter what, I choose to hold on to You. Thank you for being a good and faithful Father. Lead me down the still waters and refresh my soul (Psalms 2:2). In Jesus name, I pray, Amen.

Day 67

Pleasures in God's Presence

When our hearts are hurting, God understands our pain, and He comforts us through that pain. Remember that in the Lord's presence, we are made new. God makes known to us the path of life; in His presence there is fullness of joy; at His right hand there is pleasure in living with Him forever. God strengthens us through our hardships so that we will learn how to trust Him at a deeper level.

The Lord has never lost one! His Spirit does the transformation in us. God just needs us to show up and make ourselves available. Jesus is ready to meet you right where you are. We just have to be transparent with what we need from God! The storms of life will come, but Jesus is still in the boat with us. He will never leave. The boat may go to pieces, but you will not perish; this is not your end! What you are going through is going to come to an end for a new beginning.

"But now I urge you to keep up your courage, because not one of you will be lost; only the ship will be destroyed." (Acts 27:22)

Prayer: Heavenly Father, I thank You for Your presence, that's truly a gift. I thank You for the healing virtues that flow from Heaven to my mind, body, and spirit whenever I come in contact with You. God, I invite You in right now to saturate all of me and illuminate my atmosphere. Lord, I thank You for the comfort that You bring and the opportunity to grow in intimacy with You. In Jesus' sweet name, I pray, Amen.

Scripture references: Psalms 16:11, John 18:9, 2 Corinthians 3:18

Day 68

Emmanuel

Adoration to God is important because it allows us to praise God for who He is to us. Come let us adore Him, kneel down before Him, worship and adore Him. (Psalms 95:6)

"For to us a child was born, to us a Son is given, and the government will be on His shoulders. And He will be called Wonderful Counselor, Mighty God, Everlasting Father, Prince of Peace (Isaiah 9:6)."

There is something we can hold on to with a deep expression of gratitude in the midst of challenges because of Emmanuel which means God with us.

"Behold, a virgin shall be with child, and shall bring forth a son, and they shall call his name Emmanuel, which being interpreted is, God with us (Matthew 1:23)."

Prayer: Oh, gracious Heavenly Father, I just want to thank you for never taking your hand off of my life. Continue to orchestrate my mind, my steps, and my heart to follow You only. Open my spirit up to You Lord, even the more that I would experience You on a higher level. Bless me to grow in faith, wisdom, love, and forgiveness, and let my confidence only be found in the One and true Jesus Christ. Take me to a higher dimension of freedom in You; break through the walls I have built up so I can walk the way You need me to walk and talk the way You need me to talk.

Bless my speech to always be with grace, seasoned with salt, so that I may know how to answer and respond to people according to Colossians 4:6. Prepare me to walk in a greater realm of the Spirit with your wonderful guidance. In Jesus name, I pray, Amen.

Day 69

Bravery

Be encouraged today, no matter what you will have to encounter! In the midst of waiting to receive from God what it is that you need, the enemy's job is to distract and discourage you. One tactic of the enemy is to keep you tired and worn out, which is a strategy to keep you unproductive for God's kingdom. Be strong and courageous (Joshua 1:9), even in the face of adversity.

Repeat after me: "The healing I need is on the way. The answers I need are on the way. The finances, resources, and connections I need are on the way. The open doors I need to help me at this part of my journey are on the way. I am brave, determined, and courageous." I am a child of God, and I receive His everlasting love and forgiveness."

One of the fruits of the Spirit is long suffering, something we don't like to experience for too long, but it's necessary. God wants us to be encouraged because some things we are just going to have to go through, but we don't have to face them alone because He is always with us. Keep looking to the Lord and holding on to His hand.

Prayer: Oh wise and gracious Heavenly Father, I am coming to You as your child in need. I need strength. I need the courage and bravery to rise up in the face of the enemy. Help me, by the might of Your Spirit, to continue to press on. Lord, sometimes it gets hard down here for me. May I trust You to be my guide, and may I feel Your Heavenly arms wrapped around me. Send refreshing to my spirit, healing to my body, and restoration to my mind. In Jesus name, I pray, Amen.

Day 70

Infinite Love

As you go through this day, remember that you have been captured in God's love. What we go through doesn't change who we are to God; His love for us lasts forever. The Lord is watching over you because you are a part of God's word that He spoke into existence. Even on the not-so-good days, God is still watching over you. He has a plan to bring you out stronger and better. The temporary circumstances we go through do not mean God has permanently forgotten about us.

The past years have brought a lot of people twists and turns that have caused them to lose hope. Your new beginning can start today, not just when the new year comes around. You need the right revelation and understanding from God on how to take action. The sovereignty of God reveals that it's never too late for Him to come into your life and turn things around for the better. You can take off the grave clothes and wrap yourself in God's infinite love.

Ephesians 3:18-19 says, "I ask that you'll have the power to grasp love's width and length, height and depth, together with all believers. I ask that you'll know the love of Christ that is beyond knowledge so that you will be filled entirely with the fullness of God."

Read Isaiah 43:1-7 over yourself and put that word in the atmosphere.

Day 71

Mighty Defender

Rest in the fact that God is a mighty defender (Deuteronomy 32:4). Even if you feel like you don't have any fight left, know that God is warring on your behalf and has angels fighting your seen and unseen battles. There is still a miracle and blessing attached to what you are going through. You are able to see it when you pray for God to give you the eyes to discern His presence and His mighty work at hand. No matter how big or bad the giant is in your life, God still has the upper hand.

Psalms 62:5-7 says, "I depend on God alone; I put my hope in him. He alone protects and saves me; he is my defender, and I shall never be defeated. My salvation and honor depend on God; he is my strong protector; he is my shelter" (GNT).

Day 72

Inner Peace

The encouragement for this message is to keep your inner peace flowing so you can keep yourself in alignment with God's will.

God will keep in perfect peace those whose minds are steadfast, because they trust in Him (Isaiah 26:3).

I keep my eyes always on the Lord. With him at my right hand, I will not be shaken (Psalms 16:18).

Make every effort to keep the unity of the Spirit through the bond of peace (Ephesians 4:3).

The Lord will keep you from all harm, he will watch over your life; the Lord will watch over your coming and going both now and forevermore (Psalms 121:7-8).

My child do not forget my teaching, but keep my commands in your heart, for they will prolong your life many years and bring you peace and prosperity (Proverbs 3:1-2).

It is the Lord your God you must follow, and him you must revere. Keep his commands and obey him; serve him and hold fast to him (Deuteronomy 13:4).

The Lord bless you and keep you; the Lord make his face shine on you and be gracious to you; the Lord turn his face toward you and give you peace (Numbers 6:24-26).

But you, dear friends, by building yourselves up in your most holy faith and praying in the Holy Spirit, keep yourselves in God's love as you wait for the mercy of our Lord Jesus Christ to bring you to eternal life (Jude 1:20-21).

Never be lacking in zeal, but keep your spiritual fire, serving the Lord (Romans 12:11).

Now unto him that is able to keep you from falling, and to present you faultless before the presence of his glory with exceeding joy, To the only wise God our Savior, be glory and majesty, dominion and power, both now and ever. Amen (Jude 1:24-25).

Day 73

Plenty

As the Holy Spirit teaches you how to walk in the new you. God will also teach you how to believe for plenty and receive your provision with an open heart. After constantly having a mindset of lack, it will be a refreshing that would cause you to have a mind that believes this is your season to have more than enough. Your year of plenty if we trust and believe God will supply it no matter what this year looks or feels like.

Walking into the new you expect to have plenty in all areas of your life. A year of fruitfulness over frustration. A year of healing over experiencing constant hell. A year of dependency on God over delay from the enemy.

Scriptures for this word is coming from 3 John 1:2 Berean Literal Bible translation, "Beloved, I pray you to prosper concerning all things and to be in good health, just as your soul prospers." The Holy Spirit has also given me some powerful prayer points for the year regarding receiving our plenty. Our prayer will be based on 1 Corinthians 3:6 which tells us one plants, the other waters but God gives the increase!

Prayer: Heavenly Father, we just want to thank you for allowing us to see another year and making it 365 days of the passing year. We call forth abundant and long life for this year of plenty. We ask that you shield us from harvest thieves and anything coming in to take away from the completeness You have called us to. Thank You, Jehovah, for Your blood washing us so that our bodies and minds would come into alignment with Your complete will for our lives. May our lives continue to be planted and watered by Your holy word so that we will receive a 100-fold increase from heaven. In Jesus' sweet name, we pray, Amen.

Day 74
Divine Concern

If you want your life to be more prosperous, you have to walk in divine timing with the Lord. Every step is a praise to God. Psalm 37:23 tells us that the steps of a good man are ordered by the Lord. God knows how to locate you. He knows when to send the right help at the right time. Don't be upset with people who couldn't help you because they weren't called to.

You are not too far off that you can't be found by God. Being found by God's grace and mercy in all areas of our life. While the ground is fertile and fresh it's the perfect time for a divine encounter with God and personal visitation from the Lord. Expect God to show up for you this year like never before.

Prayer: Heavenly Father I am expecting You to show up in my health, both physically and mentally, in my finances, in my resources and connections, in my bloodline, and in my dreams and visions. Bless me to be obedient and move when you say move, go when you say go, and be still when you tell me to be still. I thank You for being Lord Almighty, I appreciate Your divine concern and care for my life.

Thank You in advance for the encounter of a lifetime that will cause the biggest shift and the greatest turn for the better in my life. Thank You for the blessings that come only from You, Lord, that make me rich and free from sorrow (Proverbs 10:22). In Jesus name, I pray, Amen..

Day 75

Sweet Heavenly Dove

Walk into this wonderful day knowing that you have already won! The Lord really pressed on my heart for all His children to be encouraged because we are walking in God's victory because His power is within us. The power comes from His Holy Spirit. *"And John bore witness: "I saw the Spirit descend from heaven like a dove, and it remained on him (John 1:32)."*

Heavenly Father, I just want to Thank You today for depositing Yourself in me so that I can live and be hopeful for another day. Thank You for communion with Your Holy Spirit. Thank You for knowing me by name!

Scripture for this encouraging message is coming from 1 John 4:4, "Little children, you are from God and have overcome them, for he who is in you is greater than he who is in the world."

Day 76
Christ The Teacher

You are not alone. God is greater than our highs and lows and will step into our situations and turn it for our good. We may experience loneliness and a yearning for something greater, but God is always with us, even to the ends of the earth (Matthew 28:20).

It's easy to look at what we don't have or who we didn't have to show and teach us certain things. The Holy Spirit is our ultimate teacher!

"And do not be called teachers; for One is your Teacher, the Christ." (Matthew 23:10)

Jesus knows life can be hard, but He didn't leave us to be powerless or comfortless. John 14:16, reassures us of the care Jesus has for us, *"And I will ask the Father, and he will give you another Advocate/Comforter, who will never leave you."*

Prayer: Heavenly Father, Thank You for seeing me through this week and bringing me into the next week revitalized and in harmony with Your sweet spirit. Help me to see You Lord as my everything, let my soul experience the fullness that only You can bring. Whatever I stand in need of Jesus, help my unbelief, and fill me with the assurance of knowing You supply my every need. Put a new fire in me that I would hunger and thirst for righteousness (Matthew 5:6). In Jesus name I pray, Amen.

Day 77

Endures Forever

Jesus is standing in the gap for you. He loves you that much! Right now many of us are facing battles we didn't sign up for but were assigned to us. Be encouraged and uplifted knowing God is still ruler over all things. Everything we go through has to come to an end, nothing lasts forever. The things of this world will all pass away, but Jesus remains, and the Word of God will never fade.

We go through sicknesses and circumstances that chose us. The enemy wants us to play the blame game and make us feel guilty about something we have no control over. Some things we just have to go through, but there is hope in our going through. Jesus is Lord over every sickness, sin, and disease.

Scriptures for this encouraging message:

1 Timothy 2:5, "For there is one God and one Mediator between God and mankind, that is Christ Jesus himself."
Hebrews 13:8, "Jesus Christ is the same yesterday and today and forever."
Isaiah 40:8, "The grass withers and flowers fall, but the word of our God endures forever."

Day 78

Love Wins

God is going to see you through it! Whatever your "it" is! Your "it" can't separate you from receiving God's love and deliverance power. No matter how big or small your need is from God, "it" doesn't stand a chance against THE ALMIGHTY ONE! The Lord wants me to let someone know He will not let your feet fail! Continue to seek and stay at the feet of Jesus. He is the one that holds the keys to that narrow gate that leads to life.

Scriptures for this encouraging message are:

Romans 8:38-39: "For I am persuaded, that neither death, nor life, nor angels, nor principalities, nor powers, nor things present, nor things to come, nor height, nor depth, nor any other creature, shall be able to separate us from the love of God, which is in Christ Jesus our Lord."
Psalm 121:3, "He will not allow your foot to be moved; He who keeps you will not slumber." and
Matthew 7:13-14, "Enter through the narrow gate. For wide is the gate and broad is the road that leads to destruction, and many enter through it. But small is the gate and narrow the road that leads to life, and only a few find it."

Day 79

Wings of the Morning

It's time to keep moving. It's easy to lie down in life's disappointments, but I am encouraging you, my brothers, and sisters in Christ, to pick up your mat and walk! I'm still learning not to be so hard on myself when I make mistakes. When I think about the sweet grace I receive when I encounter Jesus, my spirit is encouraged. I know God is not going to leave me when I fall short, but He will pick me up by His strength, so I can keep walking!

God doesn't want us walking around with our heads down, feeling defeated (John 5:8). We can be encouraged because, no matter what we have to overcome or get through, God is going to be right by our side! God is committed to us.

Jeremiah 3:14 tells us God is married to the backslider and calls us to return to Him even in our shortcomings to receive the restoration our hearts and minds need.

Psalms 139:7-12 says,

"Where can I go from Your Spirit? Or where can I flee from Your presence? If I ascend up into the heavens, You are there. If I make my bed in hell, behold, You are there. If I take the wings of the morning, and dwell in the uttermost parts of the sea, even there Your hand shall lead me, and Your right hand shall hold me. If I say, "Surely the darkness shall fall on me," Even the night shall be light about me; indeed, the darkness shall not hide from You, but the night shines as the day; the darkness and the light are both alike to You."

Day 80
Lovingkindness

There is no take backs with God. When He speaks it, it is so! What you've been through does not define where you are going! Where you come from does not define where you will end up! You have a father in heaven who thinks good thoughts towards you and who sings over you daily with the song of life when he wakes you up for another day.

People may not have treated you with the best regards and valued you like they should have, but... God will place new people in your life who are kingdom-minded and who will pour into you with lovingkindness and help build you.

Scripture references: Isaiah 55:11, Jeremiah 29:11, Zephaniah 3:17

Day 81

Sorrows Are Temporary

Thank God in advance because He causes us to triumph over every enemy. Life is all about a series of tests and trials, but God is encouraging us to be strong and courageous. This current test that you are going through, or the upcoming test, will not be strong enough to take you out! Don't let the weight of the test talk you out of receiving your testimony. You shall overcome by the blood of the lamb and the words of your testimony. You will reap the harvest God promised you.

God is allowing you to take back what the devil stole. You can rejoice today because you shall recover it all! Try not to be discouraged by the wait of when your "morning or today" is. It may come sooner than you think, or it may take a little longer than you would like, but remember, God is an on-time God! "Weeping may endure for a night, but joy will come in the morning."

Scripture references: 2 Corinthians 2:14, Joshua 1:9, Revelation 12:11, Psalms 30:5

Day 82

Burden Bearer

That spirit of heaviness has to lift up off of you! Whatever is weighing you down, Jesus wants you to rest assured knowing that He is your burden bearer. Speak the Word of God over your situation!

"Come to Me, all you who are weary and burdened, and I will give you rest." (Matthew 11:28)

"Cast your burden on the Lord, and He shall sustain you; He shall never permit the righteous to be moved." (Psalm 55:22)

"Blessed be the God and Father of our Lord Jesus Christ, the Father of mercies and God of all comfort, who comforts us in all our affliction, so that we may be able to comfort those who are in any affliction, with the comfort with which we ourselves are comforted by God." (2 Corinthians 1:3-4)

"On that day, God will remove the burden from your shoulder and destroy the yoke on your neck." (Isaiah 10:27)

"The Lord deserves praise! Day after day he carries our burden, the God who delivers us. Our God is a God who delivers; the Lord, the sovereign Lord, can rescue us from death." Psalm 68:19-20 (NET)

Prayer: Heavenly Father, I just want to thank and adore You for being so wise and holy. God, I thank You for being the solution to every answer I need. Help us to come to You first and foremost God. Teach me how to study Your word and apply it to my life so that I will overflow with power by the might of Your Holy Spirit. Give me the courage to come boldly unto the throne of grace, so that I may obtain mercy, and find grace to help in times of need (Hebrews 4:16). In Jesus name I pray, Amen.

Day 83
Complete Yes

Your "yes to God" matters, and it's important to Him. The yes we give to God puts us in divine partnership with Him.

"Whatever God has promised gets stamped with the Yes of Jesus. In him, this is what we preach and pray, the great Amen, God's Yes and our Yes together, gloriously evident. God affirms us, making us a sure thing in Christ, putting his Yes within us. By his Spirit he has stamped us with his eternal pledge—a sure beginning of what he is destined to complete." (2 Corinthians 1:20-22 MSG)

Some days will be harder than others, but even then, our answer to God should be a complete yes. Things won't always go as we planned, but our soul should still say yes. We may have to face some hard pressure, but we won't fold or go under because of our yes to the Lord.

I pray for each of us to come to a maturity where, no matter how we feel, even when our emotions try to rule over us that we will say yes to God's will and obey when the road gets cold and lonely. The loads of life get heavy, but our yes to God should come into play whenever we release our weight unto Him and get back to putting God first. The busyness of life easily creeps in and becomes first in our lives without us realizing that we have been too busy and we don't spend time with God how we used to. Jesus is calling us to get back in His word and study.

2 Timothy 2:15 says, *"Study to show thyself approved unto God, a workman that needeth not to be ashamed, rightly di-*

viding the word of truth." This scripture expresses the importance of living faithful to God. To handle God's word with care is to understand God's word. How can we carefully handle something we don't understand? Our understanding of God's word leads us to have lives that are serviced for God's work. God's word is a lamp unto our feet and a light unto our path (Psalm 119:105).

Day 84
Abundantly Blessed

Encouragement for today is *don't forget to be a blessing to someone*. Take the time out to show someone you love, work with, or even a stranger an act of kindness and love today. Things we deem as small make a big impact! When you bless others, God blesses you. The one who blesses others is abundantly blessed; those who help others are helped (Proverbs 11:25).

When we bless others, it is a form of demonstration of God's love.

"But God demonstrates his own love for us in this: While we were still sinners, Christ died for us (Romans 5:8)." The only one capable and worthy of paying for our sins is Jesus.

"God showed how much he loved us by sending his one and only Son into the so that we might have eternal life through him. This is real love– not that we loved God, but that he loved us and sent His Son as a sacrifice to take away our sins. Dear friends, since God loved us that much, we surely ought to love each other (1 John 4:9-11 NLT)."

Besides, God is able to make every blessing of yours overflow for you, so that in every situation you will always have all you need for any good work. As it is written, "He scatters everywhere and gives to the poor; his righteousness lasts forever." Now he who supplies seed to the farmer and bread to eat will also supply you with seed and multiply it and enlarge the harvest that results from your righteousness. In every way you will grow richer and become even more generous, and this will cause others to give thanks to God because of us (2 Corinthians 9:8-11)."

Day 85

God Made Me

The Holy Spirit brought a song to my remembrance that I haven't heard in about 12 years. The part of the song God sang over me this particular morning was *"God made me. God made me who I am."* So I went to look it up because I thought to myself, *"This sounds so familiar,"* but I couldn't put my finger on it! The song is by the Mississippi Mass Choir, titled *"God Made Me."*

I want to speak life into every person who reads this devotion, and I pray that you receive it in the name of Jesus. God didn't drop the ball when He made you! God didn't create you to lie in and remain in a pit! You are a conqueror! You are victorious! You won't be stopped! You are a believer! You are an achiever! You won't be blocked! There is nothing that can hold you back! What God has purposed you for, you will see the fulfillment of that very thing. Why? Because God made you for it! We can't keep talking ourselves out of what God has commissioned us for! You can do all things through Christ, who strengthens you (Philippians 4:13).

Prayer: Heavenly Father, I want to thank you for saving my soul. Please save the souls of anyone who is closest to hell. Jesus I appreciate You for being the keeper of my soul and for always standing at the door of my heart and knocking to dine and commune with me (Revelation 3:20). Lord, grant me a deeper desire for Your Word that I will grow and come into maturity to what You have called me for. Thank You, God, that Your word is my medicine. It brings life and health to my flesh (Proverbs 4:22).

Help me to see myself as fearfully and wonderfully made, no matter what tries to come up against my mind, body, and health. Thank you that I don't have to be ashamed of who I am because you have made me. Help me to see myself as the beautiful creation your word declares you were pleased with, according to Genesis 1:31. Thank you for creating me to be more than conquerors through Christ Jesus. In Jesus' sweet name, I pray, Amen.

Day 86

Momentarily

This devotion is inspired by people who often see my positivity but don't see my pain. Which I'm sure many people can relate to. As you read this devotion, I believe the poem below will minister to you. God wants us to get to the point that we are flourishing in Him.

Those who are planted in the house of the Lord, shall flourish in the courts of God (Psalms 92:13).

Growth happens in all areas of our lives, but sometimes our feelings get in the way of that growth. Our feelings can hinder us from flourishing. So if you are at a low place within yourself and think no one sees you or understands, I'm here to let you know God sees and understands. I understand because I've been there, and I am proof that if you just keep going, it's been Jesus carrying you all along.

This poem is a testament to God's saving grace and His faithfulness to us, even in life's uncertainties. I want to encourage you, the reader, that Jesus will stick by your side and see you through. No matter where you are in your journey, His grace will find you. He won't leave you, even in those moments when you feel unworthy to be kept.

Poem: Jesus Held On To Me

When the days were cold Jesus held on to me. When the nights got long Jesus held on to me. When my eyes couldn't see Jesus held on to me. When my heart was aching Jesus held on to me. When my soul was breaking Jesus held on to me.

When my tears covered my pillow Jesus held on to me. When I was restless Jesus held on to me. When I tossed and turned Jesus held on to me. When I wanted to lie down in defeat Jesus held on to me. When I was sinking in my emotions Jesus held on to me.

When my feet felt weary from life's journey Jesus held on to me. When everything was dark, and I couldn't see the light Jesus held on to me. When my life felt formless and empty Jesus provided the light and held on to me.

At times when I felt like I was barely breathing, Jesus held on to me. When I thought I didn't have anything to believe in, Jesus held on to me. When my hope ran out, Jesus led me to lush meadows and held me. When I thought my sin was the end of me, Jesus held on to me. When my mind was shattered by shame, Jesus held on to me.

When I didn't know how to walk in grace, Jesus held on to me. When abandonment screamed from within, Jesus held on to me. When my heart felt neglected, Jesus held on to me. When I wanted to let go, Jesus held on to me. When I felt forgotten, Jesus held on to me.

In my moments of desperation, Jesus held on to me. When I didn't meet my own expectations, Jesus held on to me. When I didn't know how to take the next step, Jesus held on to me. Through it all, I now see that I've been safe in His arms because Jesus held on to me.

Day 87

Lean Not On Your Own Understanding

Nothing can come between you and your God because He is your shade on your right hand. Sometimes on this journey we can't always see what's ahead because it appears to be "too dark" or unclear. Our journey may not always make sense to us based on our human understanding. God will see us through our trials and tribulations. We can take comfort in the fact that darkness isn't dark to God.

God can and will pull you out of darkness because it has to bow to the authority of Jesus. The light of God outshines darkness! We may have some hills to climb and mountains in our lives that need to be made low. God has perfect knowledge of our lives. He saw us before we were born. Every day ordained for us individually is written in God's book. Our days are laid out for us even before they come to pass.

Scripture references: Psalm 121:5, Psalm 139:12, Psalm 139:16

Day 88

No Greater Love

There is no greater love than to lay down one's life for one's friend. "You see, at just the right time, when we were still powerless, Christ died for the ungodly. Very rarely will anyone die for a righteous person, though for a good person someone might possibly dare to die. But God demonstrates his own love for us in this: While we were still sinners, Christ died for us."

God's love for us is strong like a hurricane. If only we could fully grasp onto how much He loves us. God's love is stronger than this current storm that you are going through. You are going to see your rainbow. Get ready to see that dark cloud over you turn into a cloud of Heaven.

The dew of healing is getting ready to rain down on you. God is ready for us to release our "what if's" to Him so that we can experience "God can, and God will." "What if" statements can keep us from seeing and experiencing the impossible. God can and God will statements keep us in open expectation for limitless opportunities of favor. Everything you didn't expect to see it's time to believe it shall come to pass!

God is giving us renewed strength so we can carry our cross. "For if, while we were God's enemies, we were reconciled to him through the death of his Son, how much more, having been reconciled, shall we be saved through his life!"

Scripture references: John 15:13, Romans 5:6-8, Luke 9:23, Romans 5:10

Day 89

God's Word Is A Mirror

This devotion allows us to examine ourselves.

"For if anyone is a hearer of the word and not a doer, he is like a man observing his natural face in a mirror; for he observes himself, goes away, and immediately forgets what kind of man he was." (James 1:23-24)

A mirror reflects the outside, while God's word reflects the inside. God's word illuminates our inner selves and reveals what we need to purge. What is our faith like after we say amen? Do we pick back up what we laid down in prayer for what we were believing in faith for God to move on? Or, after our amen, do we believe we shall see the favor of the Lord on our lives?

I want to encourage each of you in whatever area of your life you need strengthening in. Don't be afraid to open up to God as your Heavenly Father for Him to build you up where you are feeling weak. There is this song called *"Oceans"* that speaks volumes about this encouraging message. *"Spirit lead me where my trust is without borders, let me walk upon the waters, wherever you would call me. Take me deeper than my feet could ever wander, and my faith will be made stronger in the presence of my Savior."*

Day 90
The God Who Declares

All it takes is for one person to come into your life and show you they believe in you. They help build you up and push you past your limits. We all need people that can speak to the faith in us and cause it to arise and not people who constantly dump all of their life's problems on you like you're a garbage can.

Thank God for coming into our lives and seeing the best in us! I don't always understand why God chose me, but I'm glad He did. God's love for me is what keeps me going. God's love is why I chose to go on another day and try again, no matter how many times I "fail." God often builds us up so that we can be what we didn't have from other people. In this fast-paced world, we never learn how to purposely stop ourselves and take some time to fix what's wrong within us.

Most people operate out of the broken version of themselves that needs healing mentally and emotionally, versus the version of themselves that is working towards healing and wholeness. When God helps us to be better, for most people, it will be encouraging to see someone else coming out of the cycle of dysfunction, which will help them to desire inspiration to do the same. Others may feel that you think you are all that or that you are better than them, when the truth is, you just want better for yourself. Our encouragement on this wisdom filled day is that God sees us for who He spoke us to be before we were born (Psalm 139:13).

As you go to where the Lord sends you, He will equip you to walk into who he called you to be. When God visited His people, He addressed them as who He declared them to be, not how they viewed themselves. Oftentimes, we feel weak, helpless, not brave enough, not smart enough, and filled with so many reasons why God should use someone else.

God visited Gideon and addressed him as "O mighty man of valor," even though Gideon saw himself as having the weakest clan and being the least of his family. Get ready for God to send you an angel (Psalms 91:11) in your life to help you come into alignment with who the King of Kings declares you to be!

Day 91
King of Glory

Wherever you find yourself at this point in your journey, whether you are facing problems as high as a mountain, I want you to know that God is Lord over that mountain, and it will be made low. If you are at a low place in your life, you can still be encouraged because God is Lord over the valley and can pull you out of the lowest depths. This devotion is to encourage each reader to stand on the Word of God, even when you feel like you have nothing left. When you are at a low point, you can hold on to the truth that you have grace and mercy holding you up on each side (Psalms 23:6).

Scripture for this devotional prayer is coming from Psalm 24:7-10.

Prayer: Right where you are, lift your hands, if you are able, and pray this prayer over yourself: King of Glory fill my atmosphere. King of Peace rest in me. King of Joy, take away my mourning. King of Healing, bring forth total restoration to my mind, body, and soul. King of Power, break the powers that are trying to overpower me. In Jesus name, I pray, Amen.

Day 92

Bombard Heaven

Today's devotional message is about God's children bombarding Heaven today and sending up some thank you to God for being so good to us. Wherever you find yourself today, just tell the Lord thank you. For keeping each of us in our right minds and sustaining our bodies. We may be going through some aches and pains, but our souls can be at a place of rest because we can trust the fact that God is the keeper of our soul (Psalms 121).

Each day we wake up with the gift of life—a day we have never seen before. Every morning, there should be fresh praise brewing in us for us to hold on to throughout the day. Challenges and possible frustrations will come, but our thankfulness to God will help us keep our minds focused on Him. Jesus has been faithful and good to us, even when we didn't know how to be faithful to ourselves! Many of us can attest that we truly don't know where we would be if it wasn't for the love of God. We all share the mutual feeling of being thankful that God kept us and never left us.

Do not be anxious for nothing, but in everything by prayer and supplication with thanksgiving let your requests be made known to God. And the peace of God, which surpasses all understanding, will guard your hearts and minds in Christ Jesus. "Finally, brothers and sisters, whatever is true, whatever is honorable, whatever is just, whatever is pure, whatever is lovely, whatever is commendable, if there is anything worthy of praise, think about these things (Philippians 4:6-8)."

Day 93
The Lord Is Close

There isn't a moment in your life that God is not aware of, even when it comes to the unimaginable. He is aware and is capable of bringing you through this life filled with His strength and wisdom. When things are tough, it can feel like you are in a season where it may feel like God is far away from you, but I want to encourage you to just hold on and take comfort because He is within you and surrounds you!

One main reason why we feel like God is far off from us is because of the trouble that is surrounding us, to the point where everywhere we look, there appears to be trouble on every side. The Lord is close to those who are brokenhearted and saves those crushed in spirit (Psalm 34:18).

God has a special blessing for each of us, and I'm praying for the body of Christ to endure and stay strong to see the manifestation of blessings to come. May you experience God in a deeper way like never before, that you would share your testimony with others who need encouragement.

2 Corinthians 4:8-10, "We are troubled on every side, yet not distressed; we are perplexed, but not in despair; Persecuted, but not forsaken; cast down, but not destroyed; Through suffering, our bodies continue to share in the death of Jesus so that the life of Jesus may also be seen in our bodies."

This devotional prayer is coming from Numbers 6:24-26, "May the LORD bless you and keep you; the LORD make his face shine on you and be gracious to you; the LORD turn his face toward you and give you peace." In Jesus name, I pray, Amen.

Day 94

Act Justly, Love Mercy, Walk Humbly

God is giving us peace about ourselves! This is a time of reestablishing and realigning. Our posture is what aligns us for our breakthrough. We need to be in a posture of obedience to the Lord. We can be obedient to God by acting honorably with Him by walking humbly with Him.

We just don't need to look like "we got it all together" but we got to be right from within. How we are positioned from within takes us further than how we look on the outside. Your looks don't make you. What comes from within makes you. People judge by outward appearance, but the Lord looks at the heart.

It's not your looks that bring your fruit, it's your labor. How much work you put in depends on how fruitful you are. This is a time we need to invite the Holy Spirit in even more so that He can fix our hearts and minds so we can be found with good intentions and right standing with the Lord. Peace comes as we ground ourselves in the Word of God and learn what He says about us. When God says it, it is so!

You are fearfully and wonderfully made. God delights in you. God was pleased when He made you. You are not a failure because God is within you. You are worth dying for. You are loved with an everlasting love. You are on God's mind. You are the apple of God's eye.

Scripture references: Micah 6:8; 1 Samuel 16:7; Psalm 139:14; Zephaniah 3:17; Genesis 1:31; Psalm 46:5; John 3:16; Jeremiah 31:3; Psalm 139:1-18; Psalm 17:8

Day 95
Strangely Wrapped Gifts

It's so easy to feel like you don't know how to go forward when you keep getting knocked down. I constantly have to encourage and remind myself that I need to stop canceling myself out before I give God the chance to do the work in me. I also found myself praying and saying, "Lord, help me to take hold of the grace that you've already given me so I can go forward."

If anyone can relate to this message, I want to encourage you that God knows what you will come to Him with and what He will have to remove to make you a better person. Your life is a prewrapped gift from God. There is no need to continue to feel like you or your life is a mistake. Your efforts are more than enough; if you just hold on to what you know God gave you, you will see the effects of your efforts made strong by His strength.

Day 96
Godly Values

Only God can truly keep you. And I'm talking about the type of being kept that heals your mind when the enemy tries to take hold of it, that revives your body in ways man-made medicines and machines can't and speaks tenderly to your soul when it cries for comfort. We need to pray over ourselves that God gives us a healthy eyesight to see accurately in the realm of the spirit. Not just eyes that see but ears that's willing to listen and obey the Lord's commandments.

Matthew 6:22 tells us *"The eye is the lamp of the body. So, if your eye is healthy, your whole body is full of light."* It's time to make a daily confession over ourselves and speak life! Healing power is in our tongues.

Jesus said, "A good man out of the good treasure of his heart brings forth good things, and an evil man out of the evil treasure brings forth evil things."

Our prayer should also be Heavenly Father give me a heart after You and a heart like You and a desire to be kept by you Lord, and a greater desire to make a conscious decision to keep those things that you value as our daily values, no matter the pressure we may feel from this world.

Today we are seeing so much deception in the world, doctrines and teachings that don't align with God's values. The deception in the world calls for many to need restoration in a sense of values.

Matthew 24:24-25 says, "For false Christs and false prophets will arise and will show great signs and wonders, so as to mislead, if possible, even the elect." So that God's people won't fall away we have to be shielded by the prayers of Jesus (Luke 22:31-32) and God's power (1 Peter 1:5).

To keep ourselves guarded from spiritual deception we need an appetite for God's word to keep His values true to us and to develop sensitivity to become aware of Satan's strategies (2 Cor. 2:11).

Day 97

The Power of Forgiveness

This devotion focuses on the power of forgiveness.

"Then Peter came to Jesus and asked, "Lord, how many times shall I forgive my brother or sister who sins against me? Up to seven times?" Jesus answered, "I tell you, not seven times, but seventy-seven times." (Matthew 18:21-22)

The Lord is personally working on me in this area, and I see how there's so much freedom and grace in forgiveness. It's truly a blessing to come before God knowing that we are forgiven and loved as we ask Him for forgiveness and for Him to give us a desire to live a life pleasing to Him. It's time to let the sunshine in. Jesus helps us see the parts of ourselves that've been hidden by darkness. The sun helps us see. Jesus came to save and not condemn (John 3:17).

Walking with the Lord is more than a set of rules, it's about relationship. When you walk with Him and gaze at the beauty of the Lord, at all he has done He makes you want to do better, to live better. His forgiveness and love towards us is the basis of our foundation with the Lord.

"For the Lord God is a sun and shield; the Lord will give grace and glory; no good thing will he withhold from those who walk uprightly." (Psalms 84:11)

God is putting together the pieces of your life. God knows and understands how we feel disappointed when things don't go as expected for us. You won't be in a dark place forever. As we make one move, He will reveal the next as we go. It's not always as easy to move or take that next step whenever it is an unfamiliar place. God blesses us whenever we are obedient (Psalms 34:9-10). Pray for God to help us commit ourselves to Him.

"If someone says, "I love God," and hates his brother, he is a liar; for he who does not love his brother whom he has seen, how can he love God whom he has not seen? (1 John 4:20)."

Day 98

Path of Purity

Some days for me are not always as easy as other days. Today started off as one of those not-so-easy days. We all have those days when we need a little extra prayer and a lot more love to comfort us in our times of need and weakness. But... I know I can hold on because I have Jesus and my faith is still alive. I'm so proud of myself because I also cried today and acknowledged how I felt. I allowed myself to be open and have a moment of vulnerability.

God is still with us, even when our cross gets a little heavier to carry. This devotion is made to encourage us in our weakness, knowing that through God we can be made strong. We can lean and depend on the fact that God is the one who holds us up when we are feeling down. Even in our suffering, we have a promise to hold on to (Psalms 119:50).

"How can a young person stay on the path of purity? By living according to your word. I seek you with all my heart; do not let me stray from your commands. I have hidden your word in my heart that I might not sin against you (Psalms 119:9-11)."

Our flesh can rule over us if we are not intentional and disciplined in our decision making. Romans 8:7-8 says, *"the mind of the flesh [with its sinful pursuits] is actively hostile to God. It does not submit itself to God's law, since it cannot, and those who are in the flesh [living a life that caters to sinful appetites and impulses] cannot please God."* (AMP)

"So I say, walk by the Spirit, and you will not gratify the desires of the flesh. For the flesh desires what is contrary to the Spirit, and the Spirit what is contrary to the flesh.

They are in conflict with each other, so that you are not able to do whatever you want." (Galatians 5:16-18 AMP) *"When you go through deep waters, I will be with you. When you go through rivers of difficulty, you will not drown. When you walk through the fire of oppression, you will not be burned up; the flames will not consume you'."* (Scripture Isaiah 43:2 NLT)

Prayer: Lord, help me to stand on your word as you heal my pain physically, mentally, and emotionally. In Jesus name, Amen.

Day 99

God's Quickening Power

This devotion is a right now word for many of us. God will remove the fears attached to your tears. Sometimes opportunities of growth come knocking at our door and when we open it arrives in an unfamiliar package. Don't miss what's for you because it doesn't look like everyone else's. Be careful who you have in your ear because they could attempt to talk you out of what's for you.

The question of the hour is, "What did God say?" Have we checked in with God and asked Him for the wisdom to know what moves to make? Have we sat still long enough for God to answer us? For the earth is the Lord's and the fullness thereof (1 Corinthians 10:26). God will provide everything we need (Psalm 23:1).

In our stillness, God renews our strength; then guides us along the right path, bringing honor to His name (Psalm 23:3). God restores our failing hands. Even when you think you have "failed" and "reached the end" you can still receive God's favor over your life. God had never lost sight of you. He's with you, even through your weaknesses.

Our weakness teaches us how to be strong and have peace with ourselves. God knows the road can get tough, but He is empowering us through His Holy Spirit to stay the course. We stay the course by the quickening power of God's word (Psalms 119:25). When we examine the word quicken it can be defined as "to be revived" or "to be made alive. God's word changes our situations. God's word activates a work to be released in our lives. When God's word is absent in our prayer life, our prayers can become ineffective.

Jesus said in John 15:7, "If you abide in Me, and My words abide in you, you will ask what you desire, and it shall be done for you." An example of God's word bringing forth deliverance from scripture is when Daniel stood firm in prayer and communication with God and did not listen to the king's new law, which was *"Anyone who prayed to any god or human being would be thrown into a lions' den (Daniel 6:7)"*. "He rescues and delivers; He performs signs and wonders in the heavens and on the earth, for He has rescued Daniel from the power of the lions (Daniel 6:27)."

Sometimes we have to be placed in situations that we can't run or hide from God. We have no other choice but to pray, listen, obey and follow God. When God rescues and saves us, it can be eye opening enough for most people to change and fully live out what God has called you to do. Our past is evidence that God delivered each of us from what could have killed us. Even in our weaknesses and struggles God knows our heart and true desire that we have to know Him.

Day 100
Light up the World

This devotion is encouraging us to keep our mind focused on Jesus and less on distractions and complaining. I know this is easier said than done but God's Spirit will do the work for us as we continue to open our mind and heart to Him. Distractions can drain your energy and make you less motivated. God promises us peace when our mind is set on Him.

No matter what this life brings, I pray that each of us would learn to grow in Trust towards the Lord, who is our Everlasting Strength. God wants us to be encouraged knowing we are not by ourselves, and He will never leave us in our times of need. He knows we will fall short, but our mistakes make room for growth. It's easy to get distracted and look at our long list of mistakes but the list of God's Grace over our lives is even longer and greater.

Complaining makes you frustrated and causes you to feel unfulfilled. Unfulfillment can cause you to lean on your own understanding and could lead you to pursue a path to get what you want, which could be outside of God's plan to give you what you really need.

"Do all things without grumbling or disputing, that you may be blameless and innocent, children of God without blemish in the midst of a crooked and twisted generation, among whom you shine as lights in the world, holding fast to the word of life....." (Philippians 2:14-16).

Scripture references: Isaiah 26:3, Isaiah 26:4

Prayer:: "I pray that God, who gives peace, will make us completely holy and dedicated to Him. And may our spirit, soul, mind and body be kept healthy and faultless until our Lord Jesus Christ returns. Because God himself chose us, He can be trusted that He will complete and make all things happen concerning our life. In Jesus' name we pray, Amen." (1 Thessalonians 5:23-24 CEV)

Day 101
Being Confident of This

It's easy to be judged, mislabeled, and misunderstood by others. Sometimes you have to let people talk while God completes the work for you.

"Being confident of this, that he who began a good work in you will carry it on to completion until the day of Christ Jesus." (Philippians 1:6)

So many people have lost themselves because they wanted to fit in the "standard" to be accepted by others, when the truth is all that matters is what God says about you.

This devotion ministers to me because in today's society, it's so easy to want to try to feel like you have to prove or explain yourself to people, including family, when they question your journey because of the path you chose to take with God. When God calls you to change, it's always for the better. God sees the finality of your identity and outcome in this life.

What others don't understand about you, you don't have to force them to understand. Let God do the talking for you in this season. Your job is to be sensitive to the Holy Spirit, trust God wholeheartedly, listen for direction, walk in obedience, and unwavering faith. In your awareness and sensitivity to the Holy Spirit, God will bring you understanding for the assignment tailor made for you. Everything will be revealed in its timing. There is nothing hidden under the sun (Ecclesiastes 1:9).

"For all that is secret will eventually be brought into the open, and everything that is concealed will be brought to light and made known to all (Luke 8:17 NLT)".

Day 102
Plead in Prayer

Many of us know what it's like to be sifted and tried by the enemy. Luke 22:31 says, *"And the Lord said, "Simon, Simon! Behold, Satan has desired to have you, that he may sift you as wheat."* God has blessed me with these words of hope to encourage His people who have been feeling the pressure of being under tribulation. God is about to pick many of you up out of your hurt and bring you into a season of healing. You are getting ready to transition from being sifted to seated in glory.

It's easy to feel abandoned when you experience what it's like to be sifted, but God is about to show His people that He's been here all along. Get ready for God to do the sifting this time around, and when He removes what's hindering you, He leaves no residue or debris behind. God will separate you from the very people, places, and things that were causing you to be in bondage. Things, people, thought patterns, toxic cycles, and unhealthy habits will be sifted from you for the grace and gifting of God to come forth.

After every hindrance is removed and only you are left, you are able to take accountability. You can heal uninterrupted, without anyone manipulating your mind and decision making.

God is giving us more than a desire to do His will but the strength to go through with it until the end no matter what comes our way. In this season of sifting by the Lord, He will cause you to no longer procrastinate what's important but prioritize what's important. Action is required to make your dreams a reality. A dream without work is like a stream created to flow without water.

The water is what creates the movement and makes it a

stream. Your actions are what will make your dreams flow into reality. God has given everyone a gift to use for the edification of His church. If you are not allowed to use God's word to help someone else, then what's the point of us having a gift. In order to strengthen someone, they have to be edified by the Word of God.

The building of God's word produces a breakthrough in the person's spirit. Jesus said to Peter in Luke 22:32 NLT, *"But I have pleaded in prayer for you, Simon, that your faith should not fail. So when you have repented and turned to me again, strengthen your brothers."* God calls us to encourage one another with the wisdom and knowledge He has given us so that our faith will be strengthened during trials and tribulations.

John 4:4-44 sets the mood for this powerful poem God blessed me to write about the encounter the Samaritan woman had at the well with Jesus.

Poem: Water and the Well

Lead me to the water
Where I can go to the well and be cleansed
The water that springs up eternal life in me
A well whose water will bring me
to an expected end
That satisfies my soul that I would
never have to thirst again

Jesus knew the well was deep
but the water He was referring to was
right within the Samaritan's woman reach
Jesus spoke to her in her error,
telling her all she had ever done
He said to her "Go, call your husband"
Even though He knew she had more than one

Then He corrected her soul and made it well
Testifying with excitement
she watered into the town

The people of Samaria had ears that hear causing
them to no longer be bound because they came to
believe that Jesus is indeed the Savior of the world
Your word tells us You are seeking true
worshippers

Who will worship You in spirit and truth
Give me more of You Lord
So that I can be strengthened
Found in good standing with

what You have required of me to do
Then the disciples came urging
Jesus to eat

They didn't know His fulfillment
came by doing the will of the
One who sent Him
His work was the accomplishment
That was His meat

Though a prophet is not honored
in his own hometown
Jesus got His honor when
He sat down at the right hand
of the Majesty in Heaven
(Hebrews 1:3)

Day 103
Wake Up, Sleeper

You're going from deterred to determined! I declare and decree as we touch and agree that you are going from feeling miserable to feeling motivated! Everything the enemy tried to use to deter you, get you off course, throw you off your game, attempt to cause you to stumble, get you to quit, and throw in the towel, God will turn it around for your good, causing you to be determined to press in and focus on moving forward.

"And it will be said, "Build up, build up, prepare the way, Remove every stumbling block, every obstacle, out of the way of My people." (Isaiah 57:14)

God is getting ready to turn you from the things that've been causing your captivity so that you return fully to Him and serve Him with gladness (Psalm 100:2).

The strategies of the enemy have caused a lot of people's souls to be weary with sorrow, but God will strengthen His people according to His Holy Word (Psalm 119:28).

It's time to get in the Word. God will increase your understanding of His word as you show up with an open heart and mind to Him. This is a time where God is speaking to our spirit, calling us to wake up and walk out of our sleeping state.

"Wake up, sleeper, rise from the dead, and Christ will shine on you." (Ephesians 5:14-16)

Be very careful, then, how you live not as unwise but as wise, making the most of every opportunity, because the days are evil." God is calling every boy, girl, man, and woman to Himself, no matter if you're young or old. God doesn't discriminate because, at the end of the day, He doesn't see our skin color or our socioeconomic class. He simply sees our spirit. Our bodies will return to dust, and our spirit will either ascend to heaven or descend into hell. God cares about what our soul looks like. We can rest assured that being in the arms of Jesus is the safest place to be.

Day 104

The Power of Restoration

You know you are around the right people when you are able to grow without it being manipulated, controlled, or delayed. We have to be around people who give us room to grow freely. We are not supposed to feel bound and constricted in our relationships, especially kingdom relationships. It's important to be around people who sharpen you and do not tear you down. As iron sharpens iron, so one person sharpens another (Proverbs 27:17).

We have to be walking with the Lord in order to build properly, because anything built on a foundation other than the true Eternal Rock will crumble and fall. We can't build with our own abilities; it's not our kingdom, but God's kingdom. Yes, we are children of God with benefits, but we have to remain humble because we are not God. Trust God always. Don't trust in yourself alone. Yes, you can be gifted, but is your gift anointed by God.

You need the anointing of God's supernatural power to be on your gifts in order to be sustained and flow from Heaven. Before you move into acceleration, you have to recover as you receive restoration. You can't properly grow and move forward if you are still broken with bleeding wounds. You don't want what hurt you in the past to contaminate your future. God can give you supernatural speed, causing you to accelerate, but if you are constantly looking back, you are not accelerating but decelerating, going in circles, and looking in the past. The one who is causing you hurt isn't going to be the one who helps you heal if they don't strive towards healing for themselves.

I pray for each of us to have the right people come to our aid to help us. Speak and declare that God's helpers are coming into my life. Speak over yourself and say, "God's ability is working on the inside of me. God's work in my life is positioning me for the best." We don't want to be moving too slowly unless the Lord is leading us to be still, but if our pace is always slow, then we have to get to the root of what's causing our slothfulness. When God sends speed into your life, that's a divine intervention, and you are receiving the grace of acceleration. God is breaking the yoke of the enemy, loosing the shackles that have kept you bound, and releasing you into destiny (Nahum 1:13)."

Day 105
The God of all Grace

The Word of God teaches us that His timing is perfect. Jesus performed His best miracles when it appeared to be "too late," according to man's timing. Our greatest struggles are for the glory of God to be revealed (John 11:4). Jesus raising Lazarus from the dead is the perfect example of how, even after death, it's never too late for Jesus to roll the stone in your situation.

"Jesus, once more deeply moved, came to the tomb. It was a cave with a stone laid across the entrance. "Take away the stone," he said. "But, Lord," said Martha, the sister of the dead man, "by this time there is a bad odor, for he has been there four days."

Then Jesus said, "Did I not tell you that if you believe, you will see the glory of God?" So they took away the stone. Then Jesus looked up and said, "Father, I thank you that you have heard me. I knew that you always hear me, but I said this for the benefit of the people standing here, that they may believe that you sent me." When he had said this, Jesus called in a loud voice, "Lazarus, come out!" The dead man came out, his hands and feet wrapped with strips of linen, and a cloth around his face. Jesus said to them, "Take off the grave clothes and let him go." (John 11:38-44)

God shows us He operates above human timing and understanding. In Isaiah 55:8-9 He says, "For My thoughts are not your thoughts, nor are your ways My ways," declares the Lord. "For as the heavens are higher than the earth, so are My ways higher than your ways and My thoughts than your thoughts."

You can be at your worst, and God has the power to revive and love you back to your best self.

"And after you have suffered a little while, the God of all grace, who has called you to his eternal glory in Christ, will himself restore, confirm, strengthen, and establish you." (1 Peter 5:10)

Day 106
Jesus Provides Life

We can receive true joy when we stop looking to people to do what only God can do. Every time I cried, God restored me with double laughter and double joy. Even in the midst of attacks, God kept me in a safe resting place. Everything you need, God has an unlimited supply of it.

"Those who sow in tears will reap with songs of joy. He who goes out weeping, carrying seed to sow, will return with songs of joy, carrying sheaves with him." (Psalm 126:6)

As children of God I pray we get to a point we would believe and trust God wholeheartedly that He would bring us good things even from tragedies. No one can take your joy away from you (John 16:22).

Peace comes when we learn to accept the fact no one can snatch us out of God's hands (John 10:11). Jesus is the One who provides life that overflows with abundance, no one has the power to take your God from you!

"The LORD of Heaven's Armies has spoken, who can change his plans? When his hand is raised, who can stop him (Isaiah 14:27)?"

Day 107

Warmth of God's Love

As you read this encouraging devotion today, let the warmth of God's love flow into your heart and mind. Allow yourself some time to rest in the intimacy that God offers us through His love, which brings healing. I pray that your mind be at peace that goes above your understanding and that your whole body will sense and tangibly feel the comfort of "everything's going to be alright" that God brings through His word. It's time for us to turn the page and start fresh.

Oftentimes, we get stuck on what was, and it blinds us from seeing what is or the positivity in what could be. There's no more room on the previous pages of your life; they are already filled with what was. You can go on this morning because of the mercies attached to God's faithfulness (Lamentations 3:22-23).

We all have a past, and it takes courage and boldness to move forward. Why punish yourself for what God has already forgiven you for? Reach up, so Christ can take hold of your hand. There is a change that happens when Jesus grabs us by the hand. Just as miracles happened when He took the hand of people in the Bible, it can be so for you as you place yourself in the scriptures. God can use even the broken parts of you for His glory.

I have stuff from my past that I'm definitely not proud of, but if I had stayed stuck on my mistakes, I wouldn't be where I am today. Which is walking in this gift given by God called grace. When people try to bring up your past, or even when you feel like you can't move forward because you're stuck there, let the past be a reminder of how God never failed and not so much about how you failed. Without the old you, the new you wouldn't be present. Give yourself grace, show yourself kindness, and practice forgiveness towards yourself.

Day 108

The Holy King

This devotion is focused on encouraging us to rise and learn how to push past our fears of failing. Don't let the fear of messing up again stop you from getting back up again. A righteous man or woman may fall seven times, but will rise again (Proverbs 24:16). God is not giving up on you or the vision He has for your life. He says, *"If you continue in My Word, then you are truly disciples of Mine, and you will know the truth, and the truth will set you free"* (John 8:31-32).

Jesus died for us so that when we do fall, we can get back up, believing we are freed and forgiven. God has your heart engrafted in the palms of His hands. Your name is embedded in the palms of His hands (Isaiah 49:16). And by God's will, we have been made holy through the sacrifice of the body of Jesus Christ once for all (Hebrews 10:10).

Psalm 10:16 says, "The LORD *is* King forever and ever." Jesus is a true Servant King who makes decisions with all of humanity in mind. A Holy King who is humble and willing to serve and show respect to even those who dishonor Him.

Jesus is a King that displays the ultimate sacrifice of freedom and forgiveness (2 Corinthians 5:21). When we encounter and invite Jesus to live in our hearts (Romans 10:9), He comes in as King and reigns.

Day 109

Salvation

Do you feel like you have been drowning in hurt? God sees you and is concerned about you. "I am concerned for you and will look on you with favor; (Ezekiel 36:9). God is getting ready to rebuild what has been ruined in you, healing your broken heart and binding up your wounds (Psalms 147:2-3).

Draw near to God, and He will draw near to you (James 4:8). The hurt version of yourself has held you captive for too long. The hurt you have faced in this life has caused you to put your heart on ice. Underneath that ice lies stone, so that even if the ice melts and someone gets close to you, there is stone to keep anyone from getting in. God will give you a new heart and put a new spirit in you; He will remove from you your heart of stone and give you a heart of flesh (Ezekiel 36:26).

In order to have a healthy heart, we have to have a healthy mind. For the mouth speaks what the heart is full of (Luke 6:45). Your thoughts are what feed your heart. If you find yourself with a negative mind, which honestly, sometimes we all do, I pray that your mind be renewed and transformed. I pray that the mind, which was also in Christ Jesus, be in us (Philippians 2:5).

A true encounter with God will change your life forever. For those whose souls don't have the right keeper, you can get it right before it's too late. Let Jesus be the keeper of your soul. If you have been feeling a deeper desire for God and to grow in knowledge, learn more about who Jesus really is.

Share this devotion with someone you know it will bless. Someone you want to encourage to get to know Jesus for themselves. Romans 10:9-10 "If you declare with your mouth, "Jesus is Lord," and believe in your heart that God raised Him from the dead, you will be saved. For it is with your heart that you believe and are justified, and it is with your mouth that you profess your faith and are saved."

Prayer: God, I invite You into my heart and mind to mend and remold all of me. I have moments when I feel lost and alone with all my pain, Jesus, help me feel again. Forgive me for allowing my emotions to get the best of me. Father God, help me to forgive those who hurt me. Help me, Lord, to go forward in your love. I'm sorry if I hurt others because of my own hurt. May those I hurt forgive me, and may You restore them with healing. Fill me with your Holy Spirit continuously, so that I can overflow in You. Help me live a life worthy of You Lord, that pleases You in every way: bearing good fruit in every good work and growing in knowledge of who You are as my Lord and Savior Jesus Christ (Colossians 1:10). In Jesus name, I pray, Amen.

ᴆay 110
Identity Assured

The devotion for today is an awesome word of encouragement for those who feel like the Lord is taking them higher and need the confidence of knowing they are supported by God and not alone!

This message is also for those of us waiting for the promises of God to be fulfilled. Just because you haven't seen it happen yet doesn't mean it won't happen for you. Just as you believe in Jesus, whom you have never seen (1 Peter 1:8), believe that miracles and breakthroughs will hit your life like you have never seen before. A new wave of glory is going to come on you once you start speaking God's word with confidence.

Jesus spoke the word to the devil each time He was presented with temptation. Jesus spoke Himself to the enemy (John 1:1). He spoke His truth, which comes with power and authority. Jesus spoke the assurance of His identity to Satan. When you speak God's word to the devil, you speak the right of your identity to him, which cannot be revoked; no one can snatch you out of God's hand (John 10:29).

God is building our confidence through His Heavenly Kingdom standards and not the physicality of this world. The world's view of confidence focuses on the outer man. God's view of confidence focuses on the inner man. We have to be aware of our enemies, both physically and spiritually. We can't protect ourselves from who or what is harmful to us if we are not aware of the danger they may bring.

We have to be aware of our surroundings, even the thoughts that surround our minds. We have to pray that we won't accept the thoughts that come against us as our own and cause us to act upon those thoughts. We need wisdom and discernment to determine when the enemy's work is present.

Some people won't believe in who you have been called to be because they didn't believe who Jesus Himself was until after He rose in His identity from death and the grave. It spoke for who He was then and still is today. God is calling His followers to bring on their weapons. The weaponry of God's word guarantees your success. The Holy Scriptures are what guarantee your win!

The more you open yourself up to God and study the word, the more confident you'll be in using your weapons. Your dedication determines your destination. What you devote your time to plays a major part in your destiny. When you devote yourself to God's word, you are guaranteed to be brought to a desirable end when it's all said and done (Jeremiah 29:11). We prepare for the battlefield of life by getting an understanding and having revelation on God's word.

Prayer: Heavenly Father, help me to grow in the grace of your word. Bless me to lift my eyes unto the hills, for where my help comes from, my help comes from the Lord, which made heaven and earth (Psalm 121:1-2). Help me to rest in the assurance that You will never leave my side, Lord. Strengthen me by your Holy Spirit that I would come to You Jesus, as my connection to be one with God, being that You are the only way, the truth, and the life—the only true source that guarantees my reconciliation with God (John 14:6). In Jesus name, I pray, Amen.

ᗪay 111

Faith Brings Healing

We have a powerful early morning message to start the day with. God is greater than all your fears. You still have so much more worth fighting for.

"Eyes have not seen, ears have not heard, nor entered into anyone's heart. The things which God has prepared for those who love Him (1 Corinthians 2:9)".

Rise up this morning, knowing there are life-changing possibilities awaiting you on this day you have never seen before. It's easy for us to complain, but this morning I want us to challenge ourselves on how we will do things differently. Even if it is as simple as thinking differently, whatever it is you decide to do differently today, big or small, it's still a positive effort you will have made.

This current phase won't be your forever phase if you just hold on and keep going. Your thoughts have had you down in the dumps, but the Lord is encouraging us to come up higher in our thinking. All it takes is a thought to keep us captive and a fear of moving forward because of the "what if it can't be done" mentality. We have to examine ourselves for any doubt planted in our hearts about what it is we believe God can't do, and it's not always the matter of what He can't do, but we often don't believe it's happening for ourselves.

The wilderness exposed the untrusting and disobedient hearts of the Israelites. We often need deliverance mentally because our hearts haven't grasped what our mind knows about God and His ability to deliver.

Even when we are not physically in a place of bondage that

we were once in, our hearts can become hardened through situations and circumstances that cause us to grumble and complain against God (Exodus 16:8). When we go through struggles, it often teaches us that the healing we really need is the faith to believe God will see us through trials and bring us through successfully.

The people of Israel had great experiences of God delivering them from the ten plagues of Egypt (Exodus 7,8,9,10,11), the Passover (Exodus 12), and the deliverance at the Red Sea (Exodus 14:21-29). Even with these great experiences of seeing the Hand of the Lord move mightily, the people of Israel failed to fully trust God's ability to sustain them while in the wilderness and entering the promised land. The power of one thought influences our beliefs.

Our thoughts influence our actions. Your view of things determines your victory. The right perspective keeps you on the right path. It takes only one positive thought to believe and change your life. I pray for our restoration as God heals us from every thought that has caused us hurt and stuck with a broken mindset. That which God has not planted in us has to be uprooted (Matthew 15:13). Our thoughts sometimes feel like the truth. When the enemy attacks our mind and we are living out of the negative thoughts in our heads that seem like truth based on our circumstances.

God's word helps us to see outside ourselves and outside of the thought pattern that keeps us from moving forward. God's word draws us closer to Him when we can't see past ourselves and what seems to be hopeless. God's outstretched arm will be the hope you need to get you believing again. His outstretched arms pull us out of the bondage of hopelessness. I pray for each of you that you will experience the healing that awaits you in Jesus arms, the strength that picks you up when you are feeling down.

I pray that God will wrap you in His arms of truth by the power of His word and His Holy Spirit. May God provide shelter for your mind, heart, body, and soul to protect you from the plans of the evil one (2 Thessalonians 3:3). May you be guarded with a shield and shelter of protection (Psalms 91).

Prayer: Heavenly Father, I invite you into my atmosphere to move in the midst of my mind, body, soul, spirit, home, job, car, family, finances, health, resources, connections, businesses, projects, and goals. I invite You into my heart to turn my life around, leading me in the right direction. Give me a desire to worship You deeper, a desire to pray a little harder, the strength to fast more, the courage to live a life worthy of my calling unapologetically, a bold spirit that would proclaim your name unashamed, and a heart that believes and free of doubt. In Jesus name, I pray, Amen.

Day 112

Shifting to Greater

Step out upon the waters and watch God bless you to flow in abundance. In your stepping out, God will go before you and cause favor to cover you on every side. God is deepening our awareness of His mighty hand at work. No more functioning in dysfunction; it's time to function in favor.

God is serious about taking those who love Him to greater heights, even in our thinking. It's a bad combination for your physical location to change, but your mindset stays the same. We have to be able to think differently to function in a new place. Most people fear stepping into the unknown because of a need for control and a need to know. We have to learn to operate in the right mindset.

There are dangers in returning to what's familiar. When situations in our lives appear difficult, it feels easier to allow fear to lead us back to a place of comfortable familiarity, which is familiar bondage. Even when we know bondage isn't good for us, we still feel comfortable there because of the temporary fix it brings to what we feel we need during that moment. We feel the need to go backwards to "cope" with circumstances that are out of our control. Even knowing God and all the great things He has done and is able to do, why is it that we grow comfortable with what is not good for us?

It's easier to not step out for what you deserve, desire, or want because you are used to being let down and disappointed. However, I feel the Lord speaking to my heart, saying, "I won't let you down." In stepping out, you have to trust that you can do this. In the unknown, God deepens our trust in Him by putting us in a situation where all we can do is trust Him. When you learn to trust God, you learn to depend on Him. When you take the first step, God will provide what you need for your next steps.

Prayer: Heavenly Father, Break every allegiance of familiarity from my life. Lord, whenever I am unsettled within myself, calm and heal my nerves. Help me to hunger and thirst for righteousness so that I will be filled (Matthew 5:6). Lord, You are the living water to the thirsty (John 4:14). Strengthen me to pick up my cross daily (Matthew 16: 24-26). Be gracious to me, Lord, for it feels like I am failing to make progress, Oh Lord, heal me in every way I feel distressed (Psalm 6:2). Lord, I know in my mind that You are my helper, but help my heart to grasp on to this truth. Forgive me for looking for other outlets to be my source of healing and comfort.

Jesus, You are the only real, true, and reliable source (John 1:4). Help me not to deceive myself, Lord, by hearing your word but not following it (James 1:22). Empower me to resist temptation, in the name of Jesus. "Let me therefore continually come boldly to the throne of grace, that I may obtain mercy and find grace to help in times of need (Hebrews 4:16)." "For sin shall not have dominion over you, for you are not under law but under grace (Romans 6:14)." In Jesus name, Amen.

Day 113

God of Angel Armies

This devotion helps us focus on learning how to find joy in the midst of suffering. Life has conditioned us to worry, causing it to be our first instinct. God is breaking the conditions of this world off of us and training us to worship, praise, and give thanks to Him no matter the circumstance. We are constantly walking around inhaling, never taking a moment to breathe and exhale out all that we take in, but taking life as it comes, hit by hit, circumstance by circumstance. God is speaking to our weariness and says, *"I will refresh the weary and satisfy the faint"* (Jeremiah 31:25).

He is speaking to our anxiousness saying:

"Do not be anxious about anything, but in every situation, by prayer and petition, with thanksgiving, present your requests to God. And the peace of God, which transcends all understanding, will guard your hearts and your minds in Christ Jesus" (Philippians 4:6-7).

We can no longer avoid what is so obvious in our lives. There is no more room for discouragement in our lives. It has already taken up too much space. The God of Angel Armies is by your side (Psalm 89:8). But they who wait for the Lord shall renew their strength; they shall mount up with wings like eagles; they shall run and not be weary; they shall walk and not faint (Isaiah 40:31).

Prayer point: Lord, bless me to wait in a renewed strength. What you forgot was coming and promised to you is coming and getting ready to hit your doorstep. Take this devotion and run with it back to God so He can specify your doorstep.

Whether it's the doorstep of your health, the doorstep of your finances, or the doorstep of your connections and resources.

You may check your bank account, and money that wasn't there before will be. You may go back to the doctor, and what was there they can no longer see because it doesn't lie there any longer. Doors that you know God has promised you may have been closed off, but when you go to knock and try again, they will be opened to you in abundance. You've been throwing your faith net in the water of life and seem to be getting no activity. You are getting ready to experience overflow in those areas that you haven't been getting a breakthrough in.

Day 114

Christ Lives Forever

So faith comes by hearing and hearing through the Word of God (Romans 10:17). We can hear something and not be moved or changed by it. For believers and followers of Christ, to hear means to do. We have to hear God with our hearts, not just our ears. When you hear God with your heart, it produces an action of faith in you.

Taking action on God's Word comes after first hearing God's word. When you take action on God's Word and continue to endure through it, it becomes a lifestyle. When you become saved and give your heart to Christ, you become born again through God's Holy Word, which makes you an imperishable seed. For you have been born again, not of perishable seed but of imperishable, through the living and enduring Word of God (1 Peter 1:23).

Prayer: Heavenly Father, Thank You that through you I can live a life that never ends. Help me be a witness to those around me who are walking in darkness. I pray for your Wisdom, Grace, and Understanding to properly minister to the souls You would assign to me. As your Holy Kingdom continues to grow, bless me to be a continuous partaker of that growth. In Jesus name I pray, Amen.

Day 115
Settle in His Presence

God's love offers us a new beginning. Out of His love, He pulled me out of the sin I was living in and cleaned me up for His glory. When I look back, I don't just see a shameful past; I see my past being written off by God's love, grace, forgiveness, and mercy. If this inspirational devotion is speaking to you already, I want to encourage you to keep going because many people haven't made it to where you are right now. Thank God for not allowing us to die in our sin.

Because we are human and struggle with temptations daily, I pray for each of us to be strengthened to do right and live according to the scriptures. For it is written, healing is within the Word. I know sometimes our circumstances tell us lies like "All hope is lost," "things won't get better," "no one cares or loves you," "you're in this by yourself," "there is no way out of this situation," "if our circumstances are going bad, then we are failures," and these are just to name a few negative thoughts that come against our minds.

When they come, we have to ask ourselves, "What does the Bible say?" What does the Bible tell us about our situations and circumstances? The enemy doesn't want us to accept and believe what God's word says. "Yes, Jesus loves me. Yes, Jesus loves me. Yes, Jesus loves me. This I know, for the Bible tells me so."

When you think about inviting someone to your house, think about how personal that is. Home is supposed to be a place of rest, comfort, and security. Get excited about entering the

Lord's house, His presence is getting ready to override every form of oppression, depression, and distress that's been trying to settle on you.

The Lord is pulling you up and causing you to settle in His presence. His invitation of unconditional love and acceptance awaits you at the doorway of your soul. When you enter the Lord's house, each encounter is an opportunity for your slate to be cleaned. Knowing that God's house is a shelter and fortress for those who need safety and stability.

Prayer: "Clean the slate, God, so I can start the day fresh! Keep me from stupid sins, from thinking I can take over your work; Then I can start this day sun-washed, scrubbed clean of the grime of sin. These are the words in my mouth; these are what I chew on and pray. Accept them when I place them on the morning altar, O God, my Altar-Rock, God, Priest-of-My-Altar." In Jesus name I pray, Amen. (Psalms 19:13-14 MSG)

Day 116

Speak Jesus

This inspirational devotion gives us an identity check. You are called to the nations (Jeremiah 1:5). This is a word calling our hearts and minds to be lifted by the encouragement of God's Holy Word. The days are evil, but God is still able to accomplish and bring to pass all that He has called you to. God is meeting you at the point of your need.

The reason why things are so hard for you is because the devil fears your personal growth in the Lord. The enemy will use people and hard situations to attempt to destroy you. 1 Peter 5:8, "Be sober, be vigilant; because your adversary the devil walks about like a roaring lion, seeking whom he may devour." Your oppression, depression, and distress have been caused by the plan to stop you from reaching your full potential.

I feel the Lord in my heart saying, "This is a word designed to speak to the people's needs." Those needs of freedom from illegal attacks in the spirit realm and even in your physical life. Pharaoh couldn't kill off the newborn babies like he planned for the Hebrew midwives to do (Exodus 1:15-21) if the Hebrew women gave birth to a boy. God will send people who are after His own heart and have a healthy fear of the Lord to come to your aid. "I will give you shepherds after my own heart, who will lead you with knowledge and understanding" (Jeremiah 3:15).

All it took was two midwives for the nation to be birthed by the sovereignty of God. When Pharaoh couldn't kill the Hebrew baby boy's off at birth, he decided to make their lives hard by giving them strenuous work and burdening them with oppression beyond measure (Exodus 1:8-14). Maybe you find yourself troubled, misunderstood, lonely, and invisible. I want to speak the name of Jesus into your lives and situations.

I encourage you to just call on the name of Jesus whenever things are too hard and all that surrounds you is darkness. His name is power, healing, and life. Prepare for the Lord to break the yoke of bondage off your back and shine through the shadows of darkness pressing upon your life.

Day 117
God is Attentive

Those things that make you uniquely you—what others say is weird or different—God, the Creator of the whole world, loves you for who you are. This devotion is for anyone who has ever made you feel less than or unimportant. No more apologizing for being uniquely you. This is a message for myself. There is this song that goes, "You are so beautiful to me." That's our message for today. Be encouraged, knowing that God is preparing you to see the beauty in yourself.

Someone else can see you, but if you can't see yourself appropriately, then how others view you doesn't matter. The reason why people are so bent on being uncomfortable with you being uniquely and unapologetically you is because they haven't learned how to be themselves. I mean, really be themselves, not the show people can put on to fit in.

Keep being you. It's helping even the doubters and people who don't like you learn how to come into being their real selves and live out the part of themselves they hide from others because of a fear of not being accepted. When you are confident in who you are, you won't stress about being misunderstood.

"For we are His creation, created in Christ Jesus for good works, which God prepared ahead of time so that we should walk in them." (Ephesians 2:10)

No matter where we find ourselves, God shields, cares, and guards us as the apple of His eye (Deuteronomy 32:10). God is attentive to every moment of our lives. We only worry ourselves sick whenever we try to overplease people, overly devoting ourselves to their happiness just to be validated or approved, while we are hurting inside.

We have to learn how to fall in love with who God has created us to be. To regain passion for ourselves, it starts with taking ownership of the choices we make. When we give others the ownership to decide everything for us, it takes away more and more of the freedom that God has given us. If you never learn how to speak up, then people will think it's okay to treat you the way they do.

When we don't speak up, it only creates more room for people to invade and trespass in our lives. We have to be mindful and remember that people can't read minds. Therefore, we have to tell others how we feel if something is bothering us unless frustration builds up and that frustration can turn into anger and resentment.

Day 118

Hem of His Garment

God is coming along and putting you back together. The enemy has been playing on your emotions and getting into your mind, causing you to wander into an identity that no longer serves you. The devil wants you to be confused about who you are and whose you are. The plan of the enemy is to get you so discouraged that you won't be encouraged to go forward in the freedom Christ has called you to. Discouragement can cause you to settle in a place you were never called to remain. God is encouraging us to keep our hopes high because He's not finished with us yet!

Someone needs to know that there is more to this life because God has named you on purpose with a purpose! Your failures and weaknesses are not too hard for King Jesus to see you through. One of the main causes of our discouragement is that we often see what we need as too far off, but when we see with faith we see everything we need is right within our reach.

> *"And, behold, a woman, who was diseased with an issue of blood twelve years, came behind Him, and touched the hem of His garment. For said within herself, If I may but touch His garment, I shall be made whole. But Jesus turned Him about, and when He saw her, He said, Daughter be of good comfort; thy faith has made thee whole. And the woman was made whole from that hour."* (Matthew 9:20-22)

You won't be disappointed when you reach out to Jesus. The hem provides a connection to "the Him" who will provide all that you need *(Fresh nugget that the Lord gave me. Let it sink in)*. I feel the Lord is addressing any doubts we've been having. Doubting causes us to drift away from Him. Don't doubt; just believe. God is rearranging your thoughts about your future and rolling away the empty grave of regret that messes with your head. Keep looking up, because you have a soul worth saving. You have a mind worth keeping, and you have a heart worth mending.

ᗡay 119

Growing Pains

We'll never be able to grow fully if everything is always easy. Easy is so much "faster" and "more convenient," but being faster doesn't always mean better. Rushing can take us in the wrong direction. Proverbs 21:5 MSG says, *"Careful planning puts you ahead in the long run; hurry and scurry puts you further behind."* The danger of settling for the easy way is that you can become self-reliant.

When challenges arise, our finite minds start to fight against God without realizing it because we like to be "independent" and do things our way. Storms are designed for us to learn how to solely rely on God.

When we run out of solutions and resources, it teaches us that we no longer have to struggle to let go of self-reliance and fully turn to God because we have nothing left within ourselves to rely on. When we come to the end of ourselves, we learn to trust God instead of fighting Him.

The storms and trouble in our lives are used by God to confront our rebellion and sin (Jonah 1:4). Even when we try to run from God (Jonah 1:10), we are put in circumstances that force us to call for God's help (Jonah 1:6). This race is not given to the swift nor the strong, but to the one who endures to the end (Ecclesiastes 9:11).

Through this course of life, what do you constantly see yourself trying to rush through, just to end up repeating it over because you didn't give yourself time to learn the necessary lessons to help you grow? The essence of patience teaches us that we will make it through hardships easier when we are more calm, cool and collected.

> *"But let it be [the inner beauty of] the hidden person of the heart, with the imperishable quality and unfading charm of a gentle and peaceful spirit, [one that is calm and self-controlled, not overanxious, but serene and spiritually mature] which is very precious in the sight of God". (1 Peter 3:4 AMP)*

The power of positivity and patience has the ability to see you through anything, even your darkest day. The weight of patience doesn't always feel light (easy to obtain), but it helps you see the light (the bigger picture).

Day 120

Not Easily Broken

This encouraging message is a rich word for anyone who feels like they are at the end of their ropes or anyone who feels like the storms in their life are raging. It is a word guaranteed to bring you out of spiritual poverty. Spiritual poverty causes us to give in to the wrong emotions, the wrong people, the wrong places, and the wrong way of thinking and living. Spiritual poverty brings on a lot of hurt and shame that influences our flesh to lead us when our spirit man in the Lord should be leading us.

When you are spiritually wealthy, your soul is rich in the Lord. God is saying to us, "Hold on by faith." Holding on to our faith is like holding on to that rope. If you are at the end of your rope, tie a knot in it. Let the knot at the end of your rope be a sign for your new beginning. The knot is your hope from the cross, a reminder that Jesus sacrificed himself for your healing and freedom. The knot gives you the support you need to hang on. Tie the knot with Jesus and hang on. The knot signifies the symbol of unity between the Father, the Son, and the Holy Spirit.

"A person standing alone can be attacked and defeated, but two can stand back to back and conquer. Three are even better, for a triple braided cord is not easily broken (Ecclesiastes 4:12 NLT).

Prayer: Heavenly Father, I pray that You continue to strengthen me to do what honors You the most. Let my mind and heart be at peace, knowing I am safe in Your arms. Help me to treasure Your Holy Word, Jesus. Help me to understand your ways and lean on Your Word to be strengthened during hard times. Even as I cry out for You, God, bring to my remembrance that You are my hope, even when what I am presented with appears hopeless. In Jesus name, I pray, Amen.

Day 121
Speak to the Mountains

God has a plan for all of our lives, but He gives us the choice to make decisions, whether they are right or wrong. Some things the Lord will do quickly; other times it will take longer than we would like. The Lord is not slow to fulfill his promise, as some count slowness, but is patient toward you, not wishing that any should perish, but that all should reach repentance (2 Peter 3:9).

God is waiting to hear the voice of your heart say to Him, "I believe in You and Your word." We have to learn how to walk in partnership with God's Word because His word tells us, in all our ways, to acknowledge Him and He will direct our path (Proverbs 3:6). God is teaching us how to climb our mountains with our arms and minds open to Him and His limitless possibilities. "Have faith in God,"

Jesus answered, "Truly I tell you, if anyone says to this mountain, 'Go, throw yourself into the sea,' and does not doubt in their heart but believes that what they say will happen, it will be done for them (Mark 11:22-23 NIV).

This is a season of climbing, letting go, and holding on to Jesus. Think about how when you climb something, all you want to carry when you go up is the necessary equipment to help you get there safely and soundly. You don't want to carry unnecessary baggage. There is instruction in this encouraging word, don't miss it! Let go of the things that don't serve you and hold on to the one who you serve (King Jesus). Hebrews 12:1, "Therefore, since we are surrounded by such a great cloud of witnesses, let us also lay aside every weight and sin which clings so easily, and let us run with endurance the race that is set before us."

Prayer: Heavenly Father, help me to have full confidence in You. I know you can never fail, but sometimes I get anxious and overwhelmed with the demands of life. Teach me to rest in You. Help my heart and mind to surrender unto You, that I will allow you to lead me totally. In Jesus name, I pray, Amen.

One Look, One Love

This inspirational devotion is to encourage us when we need God to show us the path of life (Psalms 16:11). Fix your eyes on the Lord (Proverbs 4:25). In His presence there is fullness of joy, and at His right hand are divine pleasures forevermore (Psalms 16:11). All it takes is one look from God for your life to be changed forever.

I feel the Lord in my heart saying for today's encouraging message to tell the people, "I'm looking upon you with an ever-lasting love." Be encouraged, knowing God has eyes on you and hasn't left your side. All it takes is a love of a lifetime to change your life. God offers us a love that makes us want to do right. We can't remain the same when we truly experience the presence of God.

True joy comes when you know you are hearing from God and speaking with Him. There is no better intimacy than the intimacy with Jesus, first and foremost. Some people label God as if He is just a figment of one's imagination or some made-up fable. Stories of God start to become too familiar for most people because they don't push past what they have heard about God and seek to personally encounter Him for themselves.

The more we experience God, the more we understand ourselves as an important part of Christ's body (1 Corinthians 12:27). We are important to God, no matter what it is that we are going through. Sometimes it feels like when things are tough, God is further away from us, and when things are flowing well, we can see and feel the evidence of God's hand upon us. God extends His lovingkindness to us more than we know in the midst of our difficulties, and we are strengthened to go through by the hand of the Lord presently in our lives (Ezra 7:28).

Prayer: Lord God, help me to not just love You for what you can do for me, but love You because of who You are. Help me to have a satisfied love for You knowing You've already done more than enough and that Your greatest work was sending Christ to the cross of my behalf (John 3:16). Heavenly Father, You are the Great I Am over my life. Thank you for all You've done and all that You will do in Your perfect timing. Your loyal love extends beyond the sky, and your faithfulness reaches the clouds (Psalms 57:10). In Jesus name, I pray, Amen.

Day 123
Leaps of Joy

As we go through the day with this devotion in mind, may it help cause a shift on the inside of you to be encouraged and inspired. With all the chaos in the world designed to burden people with strenuous warfare, the people of God can still expect Jesus to make their hearts smile. Only God can enlighten the right people around you to serve the needs you have.

At the right time, God will send the person or people He chooses to use to show love and kindness to you. After you have seemed to face disappointment after disappointment, which has caused your heart to frown and feel sadness. Your heart is getting to shout for joy, and this will produce a different type of praise to the Lord for what He is about to do.

"The Lord is your strength and your shield; your heart trusts in Him and He helps you. Your heart leaps for joy, and with your song you will praise Him" (Psalm 28:7).

Not only is the Lord going to make your heart smile, but this next move of God in your life will give you a new song to sing unto Him from your soul. Praise is good for the heart; it allows us not to lose sight of God. Praise reminds us who our trust is in. Our need to trust in God needs to be bigger than our need to know when, where, and how God will bring us through. The devil doesn't want you to be stable and committed to rededicating your life to God. The enemy will use anything to slow down progress for God's people. We see psychological warfare being used throughout the Bible; people will intentionally mess with your mind to discourage and distract you.

"Then the peoples around them set out to discourage the people of Judah and make them afraid to go on building.

They bribed officials to work against them and frustrate their plans..." (Ezra 4:4-5 (NIV)

While you set out to accomplish God's will for your life, you will need the necessary support. The Lord works through anyone to bring about His greater purpose. God ordained helpers use wisdom, knowledge, and discernment, which stems from walking in obedience to the Lord and being in step with God's Spirit. (Ezra 5)

"The work is being carried on with diligence and is making rapid progress under their direction." Ezra 5:8)

God will bring you joy because who was once frustrating you will have to assist you in the long run.

"... because the Lord had filled them with joy by changing the attitude of the king of Assyria so that he assisted them in the work on the house." (Ezra 6:22)

Day 124

Groanings Which Cannot Be Uttered

Some days, as time goes on and the weeks pass, you may feel exhausted, like you have been in a fight for a lifetime. Sometimes our troubles feel long and dragged out. Just because life gets difficult doesn't mean that God is not able. Even in this state of being, we can thank God for being able to deliver. The type of growth the Lord has for His children is on a higher level than what the enemy cannot comprehend (John 1:4-5).

The enemy can't survive at the frequency God can take His people to. God will take us up so high that the enemy won't be able to hold on. This encouraging word is for those who have been in a battle with themselves—that version of yourself that doesn't want you to grow—that version of yourself that's scared to experience God's love or love from anyone and to have hope again.

That version of yourself that dreams of something better but doesn't fully believe it can be done. That version of yourself that takes away from the leader in you. That lousy spirit that's been causing you to settle in, always feeling low. God will not leave you in that low place, constantly beating up on yourself, but God will snatch you out of a troubled mind. The Holy Spirit will teach you to have a mind at ease.

"Likewise the Spirit also helpeth our infirmities: for we know not what we should pray for as we ought: but the Spirit itself maketh intercession for us with groanings which cannot be uttered." (Romans 8:26)

"Behold, I am about to do something new; even now it is

coming. Do you not see it? Indeed, I will make a way in the wilderness and streams in the desert." (Isaiah 43:19)

Life's disappointments have caused a lot of God's children to be limping and dragging in the spirit and barely holding on. But this new thing God is about to do will cause you to be able to walk up straight with renewed strength. God is giving out strength to do what He has commanded which is to be strong and courageous (Joshua 1:9).

Day 125

God's Invisible Work

God will make a new home in your heart. The unimaginable things you have been through will turn for your good. You may even find yourself questioning at times, "Can or will anything good come from this?." The answer is... yes! You are going to make it through because God is on your side. What's impossible to men is possible to God.

The reward you don't see is coming. The breakthrough you don't see but can feel is close is coming. The support you don't see is coming. Your condition positions you for an encounter with God. Your mess is an open door for a miracle from God. When times are good, be happy; but when times are bad, consider this: God has made the one as well as the other.

Even on your not-so-good days, remember God has a plan, and nothing can stop that from coming forth. Just because God seems quiet doesn't mean He's not working.

Isaiah 65:24 (KJV) declares, *"And it shall come to pass, that before they call, I will answer; and while they are yet speaking, I will hear."* God's silence sometimes may feel unbearable when we want to hear Him most during our time of need, but we have to trust and believe He is with us always.

"Though He slay me," says Job, "I will hope in Him" (Job 13:15). When God seems silent in our circumstances, we have to remember His written communication to us, the Bible.

Scripture references: Luke 18:27, Ecclesiastes 7:14, Romans 8:28,

ᗡay 126

Jehovah Mauzzi

Prayer: Heavenly Father, help me to start this day off right. First giving you praise and adoration, then asking you to give me clean hands and the correct spirit to take on this day as it comes. May thanksgiving flow from my heart. You are the Lord, my fortress. Lord (Jehovah), my strength and my fortress (Mauzzi), my refuge in times of distress (Jeremiah 16:19)

Speak tenderly to me, Lord; prepare my mind to be functional for this day. Every form of dysfunction and its traps help me not to fall into it. Every broken cycle of anxiety and hectic emotions, God, I give you the authority to break those things from within me. Help me not to live out this day in the whirlwind of my emotions.

Today, Lord, help me to not have a disturbed or offended spirit; help me to go with the flow of your Holy Spirit. You woke me up today with a purpose—to live in purpose, not the poison of my emotions or the poison of toxic people.

Lord, I can't do this on my own. Help me to remember and speak Your word over myself and believe with all my heart that I am an overcomer and conqueror through Christ Jesus. I don't want to be mad or frustrated today. Lord, make me over again. If things don't go as planned or when I fall or make a mistake, help me, Lord, to repent and get back up in Your name. Help me not to stay knocked down and allow life or people to walk all over me. Today will be a day of courage for me. I speak it into existence because that's who You called me to be before I even existed. In Jesus name, I pray, Amen.

Day 127
Jehovah Maginnenu

You are not a seed that the Lord will leave just hanging. God will help you to grow stronger and wiser. In order to grow, it's important to know what hinders growth. We have to be aware of our triggers and weaknesses because the enemy knows who and what to use against us so that he can attempt to have a hold on us.

We have to learn to speak peace and live with the goal in mind to be at peace no matter the circumstances (easier said than done). You can never thank the Lord too much. Your thankfulness is a form of praise and worship unto the Lord. Your voice matters to God, and He wants to hear from you. God inhabits the praise of His people (Psalm 22:3).

It's been things in my life that I know only God could have done. When you feel like you have nothing to give God because you are looking at your human inabilities or mistakes, you can give Him a Thank You. "The one who offers thanksgiving as their sacrifice glorifies Me" (Psalm 50:23).

Thankfulness turns the attention from any ungratefulness trying to settle in our hearts and minds. The more offended and distracted you are, the more you will temporarily suspend the vision and plan God has for your life to come forth. The enemy knows we can't think straight and be sound when our emotions are out of whack. Maybe you feel like the Lord is silent and far off from you, just think back to that one memory when He made a way, and you were thankful. You will start to feel Him near even more when you create an atmosphere of gratitude and not attitude.

There is a level within you the devil doesn't want you to reach. Your mind is your greatest victory you can ever win and your strongest weapon against yourself that can cause you to lose, if you let it. God, You are the Lord of my defense. Indeed, our shield (Maginnenu) belongs to the Lord (Jehovah), our king to the Holy One of Israel (Psalms 89:18).

Day 128

Adonai

Today's encouraging devotion is a reminder not to take worship lightly. God calls us to "come into His presence" (Psalm 100:2). Worship has the power to shift things unseen into alignment to work in your life. Your worship is what's going to pull you through. Your worship will beautify the art of your heart. I know you don't see a way, but keep acknowledging God. That "problem" you're facing was not meant to burden you but to draw you closer to God, taking you to a new level of faith.

Your worship is going to cause glory to fall wherever you are. Your worship has the power to take the violent winds in your life and shift it to fresh winds of God's anointing. Your worship has the ability to turn your giants into the devil's worst nightmare. Your giants are deepening your reliance on God and not yourself or your own abilities.

The enemy isn't going to understand how you can worship with your problems in front of you. Your worship to the Lord is what weakens the devil's power over your mind and situation. The enemy's weakness is God's word, the Holy Spirit, and the Blood of Jesus. You want to take the devil out, knock him out with God's word. God's voice and word ranks the highest. God is Master over all.

"O Lord God (Adonai) You have begun to show Your servant Your greatness and Your strong hand; for what god is there in heaven or on earth who can do such works and mighty acts as Yours?" (Deuteronomy 3:24)

I know what some of us are currently facing hurts, but we have to hold on because in the long run, it will help us gain more godly wisdom and patience. Which is what we will need for days in our upcoming journey. You are going to make it!!

Day 129

Two Are Better Than One

This devotion is inspired from when I went on a nature walk with the Lord. He never fails me. He uses what seems foolish or simple to some to bless others. You may feel little, unnoticed, or insignificant, but you are someone's resting place. God is walking with you.

It's easy to question why God created you, but God is encouraging His people to know you have the world's dopest and flyest Creator, which is God Himself. While walking at the park, I was able to capture a beautiful moment of a monarch butterfly landing on a coneflower. The flower could look at the butterfly and think, "Why wasn't I created to fly?" The butterfly could respond, "You were created to help the others rest and stand."

This message is for the one whose heart has been crying out because you feel out of place. God sent me to tell you that there is a place for you in this world. You were made perfectly for who and what you are meant to be of service to. Notice the butterfly landed on the flower, which was the right size not too big or overwhelming to the flower to carry but just right. You won't be for everybody and are not meant for everybody, but know there is use for you no matter what season of life you are in. Keeping growing as the flower and what you need will locate you, landing on you with blessings.

We need one another just like the butterfly needs the flower to feed on for fresh nectar. The butterfly and flower have a two way relationship. The flower needs the butterfly because, as it lands on one flower to the next, it's able to spread pollen from the time it was and reproduce. *"Two are better than one, for if either of them falls, one can help the other up"* (Ecclesiastes 4:9-10).

Day 130

Come to Repentance

God's power and authority rules over our inability. God will see you through the very thing that has been disabling you. The very things that have had a cap on you for a while, constantly limiting you, won't limit you any longer. Now the Lord is the Spirit and where the Spirit of the Lord is there is freedom (2 Corinthians 3:17).

No matter the hell you've been going through, what's for you still has your name on it. I pray for sweet peace and a spirit of rest for those who have been running on empty. God hasn't forgotten you. He's preparing you for what is to come.

Scripture for this encouraging word is coming from 2 Peter 3:9, "The Lord is not slow concerning His promise, as some count slowness; but He is patient with us, not wishing that anyone would perish, but all should come to repentance."

Prayer: Heavenly Father, heal me from my faithlessness. Let my hope always remain in you. Forgive me for any inconsistencies. Help me to meditate on Your word throughout the day and send up praises to You from my heart. Strengthen me that I will overjoy with gratitude. I pray as I sleep tonight that you will fill me with more of You. Let me awaken with a new heart and spirit in You. Thank You Lord, for taking over the very things that has been troubling me. Help my soul to be patient enough for You to come through, because I know You could never fail. In Jesus name, I pray, Amen.

Day 131

The Living Stone

This devotion is a fresh word of encouragement for those who have put a pause on what they were once passionate about. You once had a fire to create and pursue your dreams and aspirations. Whether it was a lack of confidence in yourself or maybe your circumstances prevented you from being as successful with progress because your hands were already too full. "It's time to pick your pen back up."

The time is now to get started on whatever it is the Lord has charged you to do. Whatever your "pen" is, pick it back up. Your story is not over. There is work for you to do! This is the year of commitment; it's not the time to give up on yourself now. Is your heart and mind ready to say, "I'm not leaving out of this year empty-handed, with just a whole bunch of reasons why I never got started or got started but haven't finished."

God is serious about you and what He placed on the inside of you. You might have to cry, but get started. You may lose some people along the way, but get started. It may feel like it's just you against the world, but get started. You may not feel good enough within yourself, but get started. I know what it's like to go through things that have crushed my soul, that have caused my self-esteem to be low, when I felt like I couldn't love myself, to give myself up to people when they didn't value me only what I could do for them. BUT GOD!

Let God heal you so you can get started and do the best you can. God sees the broken parts of you and has His arms open to hold you close. You don't have to be afraid or ashamed of your brokenness.

"As you come to him, a living stone rejected by men but in

the sight of God chosen and precious, you yourselves like
living stones are being built up as a spiritual house, to be
a holy priesthood, to offer spiritual sacrifices acceptable
to God through Jesus Christ." (1 Peter 2:4-5)

Prayer: Heavenly Father, help me to not be slothful and disobedient in pushing forth towards my destiny. Help me to see myself how you see me, Lord. Remove the spirit of identity confusion and barrenness. With Your help, God, let this be a productive year and not another year where I come out empty-handed. Lord, help me to believe that You can do what you said You are going to do through me. Help my unbelief. In Jesus name, I pray, Amen.

Day 132

Crush Satan Under Your Feet

This devotion is focused to build our hope in the Lord through a word of encouragement, scripture, and a short prayer. God is holding you together. You may feel like you are breaking but you are not going to go under!

"The God of peace will soon crush Satan under your feet. The grace of our Lord Jesus be with you." (Romans 16:20)

"Yet I am confident I will see the LORD's goodness while I am here in the land of the living. Wait patiently for the LORD. Be brave and courageous. Yes, wait patiently for the LORD." (Psalms 27:13-14 NLT)

Prayer: Oh Gracious, Wise and Loving Father, help me to trust in Your hand in the dark seasons. Lord, help me to bless Your name and be thankful no matter what time of the day it is. Thank You God for loving me unconditionally forever. In Jesus name I pray, Amen.

Day 133

On A Hill There's A Cross

This is an encouraging devotion for all of us, no matter where we are in the Lord. Your assignment is greater than your response to negativity if you are so busy responding to every offense that takes you away from working towards your goals in God.

I am in a season where God is training me how to respond back to people His way (not Tiaina's way) even if that means not saying anything at all. The importance of silence teaches us how to pray and be still. The scripture tells us, *"A gentle answer turns away anger, but a harsh word stirs up wrath. The tongue of the wise makes knowledge attractive, but the mouth of fools blurts out foolishness."* (Proverbs 15:1-2 CSB)

The Lord made it clear to me while He spoke to my heart through this current circumstance I'm going through that the battle is not always the other person, it's my response. Our responses can truly be a battle for us if we haven't reached the spiritual maturity God is calling us to. God is leading His children to a place that He is calling us to have dominion over in our minds and where He has granted us access to.

Prayer: Heavenly Father, help me not to be a fool with my words, even when someone else's words hurt me. I pray for a covering over my memory bank so that I will only replay your goodness and not the offenses I have taken from people. Help me to do unto others how You do unto me; showing others love, grace, mercy, another chance, and forgiveness.

Because I belong to You Jesus, help me to love wholeheartedly, forgive wholeheartedly, and show grace and mercy wholeheartedly. Help me, according to Exodus 14:14 to be confident that You'll fight my battles if I be still. Bless me, Holy Spirit to walk in the dimension of grace You have called me to with peace and patience. When attacks are sent to frustrate and distract me, help me to look to the hill where Jesus sacrificed His life for me on the cross (Mark 15:22-32).

Thank You, Lord, for allowing me to be sane when circumstances around me scream insanity. Lord, before I leave my house in the morning's, I'm asking You to go ahead of me in my job and anywhere else I go. Father, if anyone says anything to me that isn't in alignment with Your word, help me to maintain Your word, peace, wisdom, and understanding so I can be in alignment with You. Bless me to forgive and not to hold any grudges. Bless me to not entertain what is not in alignment with You, Jesus, and keep me at the foot of the cross, in alignment with Your word, so I can humbly do Your will. In Jesus name, I pray, Amen.

Day 134
Jesus Calms the Storm

Our encouraging message for today is "don't sink!" Be determined not to hit the bottom, in spite of the severity of the winds and waves trying to hit your life. You may be in the eye of the storm, but we have to learn how to act on the word God gives us versus acting on entertaining the schemes and plots the enemy are sending our way. Some fights wouldn't even be a battle if we learn to use wisdom and kill the enemy with silence (stepping on my own toes).

Certain demonic spirits live to thrive in chaos. If things are not messy and drama filled some people can't stand the fact of peace and unity. The devil comes to steal and eat up the word God has planted in you. Every time God places a word on my heart, here comes the enemy trying to get me off focus, but I know I have to remain steadfast and self-controlled. It's not always easy, but I thank God for working on me.

An example of scripture for this inspirational devotional: Peter started to sink in the water because the wind was blowing hard; fear filled him, and he took his eyes off Jesus.

"Lord, if it's you," Peter replied, "tell me to come to you on the water. Come," he said. Then Peter got down out of the boat, walked on the water and came toward Jesus. But when he saw the wind, he was afraid and, beginning to sink, cried out, "Lord, save me!" Immediately Jesus reached out his hand and caught him. "You of little faith," he said, "why did you doubt?" And when they climbed into the boat, the wind died down. (Matthew 14:28-32)

Day 135
Beautify the Meek

Sometimes all a person needs is to feel love and genuineness from someone. It's amazing what a "small" act of saying, "Hey, you were on my mind, and I wanted to send some love your way," will do for a person. God's love is true and pure, available to you without reservations. This is a season where God is healing our mentalities, and it's going to start with His love.

Expect to be strengthened by His love, mended by His love, guided by His love, shielded by His love, and covered by His love. You may find yourself feeling broken and beaten, but you can still be beautified by His love.

"For the Lord takes pleasure in His people: He will beautify the meek with salvation". (Psalms 149:4)
"Your love, LORD, reaches to the heavens, your faithfulness to the skies. Your righteousness is like the highest mountains, your justice like the great deep. You, LORD, preserve both people and animals. How priceless is your unfailing love, O God! People take refuge in the shadow of your wings." (Psalms 36:5-7)

Day 136

Rejoice

God will take you from feeling useless to showing you just how useful you are to Him and His kingdom. It's easy to be in a battle with yourself and feel like, "I just can't do anything right." I feel the Lord saying to my heart, "It's time to rejoice, you were made on purpose with a purpose." This is the day that the LORD has made; let us rejoice and be glad in it (Psalm 118:24 ESV).

Now is the time that God wants to pull His people out of feeling sorry for ourselves because of our faults. Our faults and mistakes won't stop God from fulfilling in us what He has ordained for us to do in advance. For we are God's handiwork, created in Christ Jesus to do good works, which God prepared in advance for us to do (Ephesians 2:10 NIV).

Day 137

Posture of Prayer

God didn't bring you this far to leave you. After a day of challenges and seemingly disappointing experiences, by the time we get home, most of us are just ready to lay down, relax, and maybe even attempt to get some rest. As you prepare for bed, I encourage you to pray over your pillows, the place where you lay your head. A scriptural prayer that you can pray, declaring God's goodness over your life.

"I will go before you and will level the mountains; I will break down gates of bronze and cut through bars of iron. I will give you hidden treasures, riches stored in secret places, so that you may know that I am the LORD, the God of Israel, who summons you by name." (Isaiah 45:2-3)

This scripture encourages us to trust God enough, as Abba Father, to level things out for each of us so that we won't continue to worry ourselves sick. After prayer, meditate on that one scripture that speaks to your need from God.

There is a rest the Lord is giving out, and He's meeting you at your point of release. Believe that the thing that you are giving to God is going to work out in your favor. As you position yourselves in a posture of prayer, I pray for plenty of rest, an overflow of peace, and protection. I know what it's like when it seems like the days are getting harder and harder, but I feel the Lord saying, "I won't let you lose sight of Me or faith in Me." Sleep tonight, knowing you are secured in His arms.

Day 138

Fix Your Gaze on Jesus

Your growth in Jesus is going to take you from a weary to a well-watered land. We can't be so quick to deceive ourselves into thinking a way is right just because it feels good to us. God is encouraging us to follow His lead on a courageous, integrity filled and honest path for our lives. "Let your eyes look straight ahead, fix your gaze directly before you. Give careful thought to the paths of your feet and all your ways will be established" (Proverbs 4:25-26)

God has to clean the lips of our hearts because even when we don't speak with our mouths, our actions which flow from our heart will speak for us. We can't expect God to bless what we continue to be irresponsible with. Pray for God to find you trustworthy with what He has currently placed in your hands. While in transition from preparation to receiving, we have to come out with more wisdom and sensitivity to the voice of the Lord.

We have to be able to manage the little we have in order to manage what is to come. There is still hope and encouragement for you even when you know which way to go. Don't let your present tears continue to be the same tears from previous years.

Day 139

Take Up Your Position

Some of us are in upcoming battles and it can even feel that the way to go is unclear. What you are up against may appear bigger than you but it's not greater than God.

"Do not be afraid nor dismayed because of this great multitude, for the battle is not yours, but our Lord Jesus Christ." (2 Chronicles 20:15)

God will give you courage to face whatever it is you are up against because He is with you! There is divine instruction that will bring forth your deliverance from this message. "You will not have to fight this battle. Take up your positions; stand firm and see the deliverance the Lord will give you (2 Chronicles 20:17)."

We are guaranteed wins whenever we build ourselves up in the Spirit. The Holy Spirit is teaching us how to go into a physical battle with a spiritual weapon of praise (2 Chronicles 20:21).

Your praise is going to bring your enemies into a defeated place and you into a delivered place (2 Chronicles 20:22).

Day 140

Sow in Tears

There are going to be people and situations sent to crush you and your call from God. Sadly, sometimes it's even people in the church who think their actions towards you will stop God from finishing what He started in you. God knows all that you will have to go through with people and knows what it takes to push you to your next level. You may feel like you are in a tight space but know you are covered by a God who will never leave you nor forsake you.

The truth is healing hurts especially emotionally healing, but when you come out on the other side you'll see it will all be worth it. In the Spirit I see many hurt people waving a white flag of surrendering to God's will because you have no fight left all you have is your tears. You've been crying day after day and going on putting your smile on even when you feel like you are about to crumble.

When God takes you through the process of healing from your hurt no matter what form of hurt it is, it's not going to be the way we think it should be. It's easy to feel like "Lord, don't let another person hurt or let me down", the truth is this world, and people's hearts are getting darker and colder. Everything we thought we have seen and known, as we go on we can realize we haven't seen anything yet. I know what it's like to be in a room full of people and sometimes, it's church people at that but yet be suffering in silence. If you have found yourself hurt, God sent me to remind you that He is still the keeper of your soul. People and leaders may have let you down, but God has not overlooked you. You may have gotten off track but there is hope for you because you're still being considered and sought after by the lord Jesus Christ himself.

God is still able to send people you don't know to your aid to help bring you to the place of deliverance and healing He desires for you to have. God knows many of His people have been feeling sad and depressed, but the Holy Spirit will still fill you up with a spirit of courage, peace and contentment, no matter what's going on. You're not by yourself, your whole mind, heart, body and soul is in God's hands!

Day 141

Thank You Lord

Have you ever been at a point in their journey where you have a need then anxiety and worry try to kick in because of the weight of the wait for God to move on your behalf? Or that moment when you reflect back over your life at those times when God provided a need you didn't even know you needed, but as you look back and realize things could have been worse, but God stepped in and made a way.

Wherever you find yourself presently, God placed on my heart for the focus of this devotion to just tell Him Thank You. Jesus has been better than good to me, and the truth is we often create our own burdens when we walk around carrying the weight of things that God is waiting for us to release to Him.

We get beat down and discouraged because we are trying to look at our situations with our own understanding instead of trusting that God's understanding is higher than ours and in His timing all things will work out. This is the hour like never before that we need to pray for the development of maturity and discipline so that even when we don't understand what God is doing, we can still Trust Him.

When anxiety and worry come, just say, "Thank You Lord". You have more bills than you do money, "Thank You Lord". Seems like all hell is breaking loose around you, "Thank You Lord". Your constant "Thank You Lord" while you're waiting for God to come through is going to shift some things in you and around you. You've already prayed and done all you know to do, now it's time to stand. We often don't know how God is going to come through on our behalf, but we just know to trust that He will come through.

God has already declared many things over our lives, yet circumstances are opposite of what God has spoken and promised. God doesn't want us to worry ourselves sick and be in constant war with one another when we all are going through our own personal battles.

Don't allow your circumstances to cause you to fight with people who are not your enemy. My prayer for all of God's people is that we would yield to the Holy Spirit and go about handling situations the right way. We know when times are hard it seems like we are taking the worst hits.

You may feel beat down but in the name of Jesus you will rise because when you belong to God. He won't allow you to stay down for too long! There is purpose in your pain!

"We are pressed on every side by troubles, but we are not crushed. We are perplexed, but not driven to despair. Persecuted but never abandoned by God. We get knocked down but not destroyed (2 Corinthians 4:8-9)".

Prayer: Heavenly Father, I pray that my worship will always flow from a pure and sincere place. Let the thankfulness of my heart and my expression of gratitude be bigger than mumbling and complaining. Jesus, fix my gaze upon You so that I won't have to compare, be envious or upset about someone's else's walk whenever you are blessing me in my own special way. Fix my heart to be postured towards all of who You are and all of who You say I am. In Jesus name I pray, Amen.

Day 142

Heart Matters

The Lord has given me an uplifting word on the matters of our heart. Keep serving and putting Jesus first, only He can affirm your work that you do and make your efforts successful. God can take you from having a heart of brokenness to a heart of wisdom.

I know this is a sensitive time for many people and your heart needs to be reassured in the Lord. A cheerful heart is good medicine, but a broken spirit saps a person's strength. God comforts us by His word and love when we are feeling anxious. When anxiety was great within me, Your consolation brought me joy. God is greater than our feelings and He knows everything.

Scripture references: Psalm 90:17, Psalm 90:12, Proverbs 17:32, Psalms 94:19, 1 John 3:20 NLT

Prayer: Heavenly Father, remove vexation from my heart, cast off distress from my body (Ecclesiastes 11:10). Help me to love you God and love people. Let what flows from within me only be good fruits that come from You.

Forgive me for those I have wronged and hurt and bless me to forgive others who have wronged and hurt me. Let me draw near to You with a true heart of in full assurance of faith, with my heart sprinkled clean from an evil conscience and my body washed with pure water (Hebrews 10:22 ESV). In Jesus name I pray, Amen.

Day 143
Search Me, Oh God

You are getting back up again, as long as you are alive there is still a mandate over your life from Heaven. You may feel beat down, but you will rise again because of the resurrection of Jesus (John 11:25). He got up so we have to get up again. God knows we make mistakes, and all have growing to do but this is not the time to put yourself on pause and hang up the gloves on yourself.

As often as we should pray the prayer "Search me, Oh God" (Psalm 139:23), it's easy to get afraid when we see parts of ourselves we didn't know were a problem. There are habits and ways of thinking that we have developed over time. God can still lead you to the path of everlasting life (Psalm 139:24).

When God shows you the areas about yourself that need growth, don't be ashamed, and constantly condemning yourself, but let God love you and lead you to a fruitful and peaceful path. Don't draw back from God as your Heavenly Father because He still loves you with an everlasting love.

Late in the midnight hour God can turn your mind around, your situation around, your emotions around, whatever you need around. The cuts of being pruned are not to hurt you but to help you be better. Those branches that are being removed from you because they are not useful in producing good fruit (John 15:2), the process doesn't feel good, but I pray that each of us would have a courageous enough heart to let God have His way to work through us.

Prayer: Heavenly Father, I pray that You would continue to teach me to rest in you, and continue to clean up my heart and mind. Allow me to allow You to free me from my hurts as I take one day at a time. Help me not to draw back from You even when I know I messed up. May Your Holy Spirit always remind me that I am loved and nothing can get in the way of that (Romans 8:38-39).

I pray that you will heal every person I hurt through my words or actions. Forgive me for any wickedness, bad attitudes, or ungodly ways that have been in me. Help me to live out this life as your Earthen Vessel as you mold me into the person you designed me to be. Thank You for the grace to go forward. In Jesus name I pray, Amen.

Day 144

His Eye is on the Sparrow

This encouraging devotion focuses on those who are hurting. God watches over the birds of the air and the flowers in the fields, attending to them with such care. Your life is more precious than a bird. Even the very hairs on your head are numbered and known by God. Your story will end in victory because God has plans to prosper you and not to harm you.

Jesus cares about your pain and suffering. I know what it's like to feel like you can't see past your hurt, but I pray that in your pain and suffering, the Lord will open your eyes to help you see your blessings in disguise. There are many times in my journey where I feel helpless, but God is teaching me to look at my life's situations this way: "How can you help someone if you don't know what it's like to need help?"

The Holy Spirit spoke to my heart plainly and said, "Someone's deliverance lies in your obedience. Your belief in God is going to bring many others to the belief that Jesus Christ is truly the only Lord and Savior." If this message is speaking to you, be empowered, knowing there is a place for you in the Father's house. When I'm the hardest on myself, God always sends someone in my path to remind me that I'm alone and that I'm not the only one battling certain things. He sends people into our lives when we are feeling low and need encouragement to be uplifted. He also sends people into our lives when we are on a high mountaintop and need to be humbled. But through it all, whatever deliverance we need is possible because we shall overcome by the blood of the lamb and the words of our testimony.

Scripture references: Matthew 10:31, Matthew 10:30, Jeremiah 29:11, John 14:2, Revelation 12:11

Day 145

Power of the Holy Spirit

You may find yourself constantly trying to swim and wallow in the waters God has called you to walk on. By faith, God will cause you to walk over the exact things designed to take you under. My prayer for all of God's children is that we will see the physical manifestation of every yoke trying to continuously bind us to depression, anxiety, hopelessness, isolation, constant agony, suicidal ideation, worry, overthinking, negative thinking, replaying the past, bitterness, unforgiveness, jealousy, separation, strife, vengeance, and be burned and broken by the fire and power of the Holy Spirit.

May God prepare our hearts and minds as He exposes every hidden agenda and evil altar built against our lives. The weapons may form, but they won't prosper. Don't give up on God because things are forming against you. His Word tells us that many are the afflictions of the righteous—not some or a little bit, but many! You may even question and say what is the guarantee that I'm coming out of this, but God's word is your guarantee that your deliverance is coming! (Psalm 34:19)

Prayer: Father God, I need You to show me the way forward. As You show me the way, help me to step out on faith and pursue the path you have laid before me. Help me to listen to Your voice as I walk through any challenging circumstances. Bless me to have a teachable spirit. Help me to give myself fully to Your will and ways Lord. In Jesus name I pray, Amen.

Day 146
Saved by Grace

Whatever life is throwing your way, just know it won't always last. Anything that you are facing can be fixed! The enemy may try to throw in your face the amount of time you have been dealing with that circumstance, but God wants us to be encouraged to not let the accuracy of the facts of how long we've been facing the circumstance become a permanent belief that we will be in that situation forever.

In time, you will see God's mighty hand of deliverance. You may be weeping now, but you will rise up, rejoicing! No matter how deep the hole is that you're in, our Lord Jesus is always fighting on our behalf, and the Father is working behind the scenes. God will not let His people end it all or let you lose your mind through this. Trust that God will keep you through whatever your "this" is.

Day 147

Broken for the Glory of God

When your eyes are healthy then your soul is also healthy too. "The eye is the lamp of the body. If your eyes are healthy, your whole body will be full of light. But if your eyes are unhealthy, your whole body will be full of darkness. If then the light within you is darkness, how great is that darkness (Matthew 6:22-23 NIV)."

Healthy eyes also mean knowing when to be silent, when to move on, being able to forgive others, recognize your own hurt and how to move forward from it. Hurt can sometimes leave us in a bound state if we don't undress it. We can't keep dressing up our hurt trying to make it look pretty when it's making us ugly on the inside.

Prayer: Father God, my heart has been weighed down and I need You to strengthen me to put Kingdom things first. I need You to restore my eyes and allow me to fully see Your light again. Help me to see clearly today like never before. Let me not miss another day of Your glorious wonders all around me.

Anoint me even the more Lord with Your spirit of wisdom and maturity that my eyes may see, and my ears may hear, that my decision making and how I move will be according to Your Spirit and not my emotions and flesh. Bless me to longer be a slave to my hurt. Forgive me for every time I allowed my eyes to lead me in an ungodly manner. Thank You for the grace to go forward. In Jesus name I pray, Amen.

Scripture references: Psalms 38:10, Mark 8:25, Proverbs 20:12

Day 148
Watch and Pray

Constant frustration is a harvest thief sent to steal your joy. You ever get to the point where you are examining your circumstances and say, "Something's gotta give. I don't want to be mad or bothered every day." Your frustrations can be lessened when you realize that you are not wrong for protecting your personal space and learn how to protect your personal space.

Protecting your space is protecting your heart. The word tells us above all else to guard your heart (Proverbs 4:23). God knows how easy it is for our heart to be troubled by the world, people, and our circumstances. Our frustration can cause us to hurt others by the tone of how we speak when it comes out. Our encouragement for today is reminding us to just pause for a little bit. Our pause will keep us from having a firecracker response.

Lord knows it is hard for me to come down after I get riled up, so we have to know when and how to avoid situations from escalating and getting out of hand. We have to yield to the Holy Spirit to allow the work in us to be done, taking us from a lifetime of frustration to a lifeline of fixation by prayer. Our first response is usually to act off of our frustration, but I've been finding myself praying, "Lord, let me not allow frustrations to get me in trouble or out of character. Teach me how to watch as well as pray (Matthew 26:41)." The temptation comes when we want to give people a piece of our mind, knowing we are supposed to let the Lord fight our battles. The temptation is to seek vengeance to get that person to feel how you feel.

Growth and maturity is having the opportunity to make the person who hurt you feel how you felt, but you choose to be a peacemaker anyway (Matthew 5:9).

Prayer: Father, before I do anything to bring disgrace and dishonor to Your name, help me to walk away with peace knowing I have already won."

Day 149

Get A Grip

Where you are currently is shaping you for where you're going. Do not despise these small beginnings (Zechariah 4:10). Jesus is your Partner in this journey (John 15:15). There is treasure in "small beginnings". As you continue to journey on you will see that your "small beginning" is teaching you how to get a grip. If you can handle the struggles and challenges in your small beginning, then you can handle anything that comes your way later down the line, through the strength of God.

In small beginnings, you gain wisdom, your discernment is sharpened, you learn how to hear the Lord, you build a solid foundation with God, you become more grateful, you become more patient, you gain a heart for God's people and the things of God, you learn how to preserve your integrity, and you learn how to get a grip over your mind and emotions, which leads you to become more mentally and emotionally stable for where you're going.

Put a praise on your small beginning. Your praise will lessen your anxiety. Your praise will lessen your complaining. Your praise will add to the joy for where you are currently. Your praise will add to the joy for where you are going.

Day 150
Reveal the Ram

Sometimes what we see as an Inconvenience is God intervening. We can go to the right place at the wrong time, with the wrong mind and attitude.

Prayer: "God help me to not show up too early on the timing I feel is best when you are clearly showing me to slow down, gather my thoughts and yield to Your Spirit". God knows the road we must travel (Job 23:10).

The Lord will place someone there for you to encourage you, to cover you, and to help you. I know it seems like you've been pushed against the wall, from everyone constantly wanting to take, take, take and want you to give, give, give with no one to pour back into you. When no one else is in your corner just know the favor of God is in your corner. Out of your willingness to be obedient to God will bring you many blessings.

To give God back what you truly treasure is a test. What you need is already there but in His timing He will reveal the ram. Your obedience in being willing to go where the Lord sends and give what He is asking of you to will cause God to respond by revealing the ram.

First came the word that God gave Abraham, then Abraham responded with obedience to the command given by God and after Abraham obedience to sacrifice his son Isaac as a burnt offering on a mountain. The Lord saw his heart towards Him, so God provided a ram to sacrifice instead of his son Isaac.

Scripture references: Genesis 22:2, 3, Genesis 22:18, Genesis 22:13

Day 151

Strange Favor

This devotion will start with me sharing a testimony then the word of encouragement.

Testimony: On this particular day I got off work I had two bills I needed to take care of. So when I went to pay what was due, the cashier started by asking me how I was doing and how my day was. I told her I had been at work since 5 am and it was 5:15 pm when I got over to where she was. She told me how much my bill was, and I gave her my card.

After she explained how her day was going she ended our transaction with a warm smile after saying "God bless your heart, go home and get you some rest." Fast forward as I am getting ready for work the next morning and packing my bag to make sure I have everything, the receipt from the day before was laying right next to my bag. I was getting ready to ball it up and trash it but when I looked down I noticed that the lowest bill was paid by me, and the other bill was paid but stated $0.00 on the receipt.

The Lord showed me favor even though I had the money to pay for it, she took care of the highest bill for me. The Lord continues to show me that there is no where I can run outside of Him, that He doesn't see me and is watching over me. "And low, I am with you always, even unto the end of the earth" (Matthew 28:20).

This may not mean much to some, but it means a whole lot to me especially being that I did not know this lady and she showed me kindness and sowed into me. It feels nice when you are on the receiving end especially since I am always sowing and encouraging others.

Word of Encouragement: Expect for God to show you strange favor in the most unexpected moments. "Therefore know [without any doubt] and understand that the Lord your God, He is God, the faithful God, who is keeping His covenant and His [steadfast] lovingkindness to a thousand generations with those who love Him and keep His commandments;" (Deuteronomy 7:9 AMP).

I know times are hard, but I want to encourage someone to let you know that God can still move and work on the hearts of people just to bless you. I know physically it can look like you are by yourself, but God knows when to come at the right to have people you do not know come to your aid (Isaiah 55:5).

Day 152

Display of His Splendor

I pray this devotional inspiration blesses you and helps bring in a faith filled and uplifting day. No matter who or what you're up against just know you are unstoppable and with God on your side. You may feel like your troubles will break you, but God will hold you up (Isaiah 41:10). "And provide for those who grieve in Zion-- to bestow on them a crown of beauty instead of ashes, the oil of gladness instead of mourning, and a garment of praise instead of a spirit of despair. They will be called oaks of righteousness, a planting of the LORD for the display of his splendor (Isaiah 61:3)".

For some people, your faith will be a threat, instead of your faith being a teacher encouraging them to go deeper with God. People will make comments like, you church going people act holier than thou but how can anyone judge your relationship with God just because they don't choose to put in the work and effort that you do. People will do anything they can to make slick comments to provoke you, try to oppress and control you because they are jealous of how strong your spirit is in the Lord.

Those same people will look at you and say "Oh, and you're supposed to be a Christian." They will try to break your spirit and then you wonder why when you get around certain people your spirit feels unsettled. Because they have already spoken word curses into the atmosphere, and you can feel that something is wrong. People want you to take your eyes off of God and they will do and say things to try to fault you then when you stand up for yourself they play victim just to manipulate you to feel like you are a bad person, like you are not who God says you are.

People may try to purposely break you but that's only going to cause God's glory to shine on you more as He continues to make and mold you. But there is hope if you don't get anything else out of this encouraging message remember that even the not so good days are a gift from God. It's our duty as Children of God to learn how to still be able to find Him through everything we would have to go through. The opposition against you wants you to be so disconnected from God by what's going on to the point that you shut Him out.

No matter what's going on around you, the Lord will still anoint you with His presence when you draw closer unto Him. The pain of where you are is teaching how to rejoice for where you're going. Because when you get to where you're going, you are going to look bad and just be glad Jesus brought you through. Even on challenging days there is always something to be thankful for.

There may be pain in you but there's still a praise in you. Give in to your praise and not your pain so God can have His way in you. If you can relate to this devotion my prayer for you is that God would continue to wrap His ever so loving arms around you. I'm praying that when you give what's burdening you to God that you won't pick it back up, that the Lord would move in your heart and make room for His splendor. I pray for a supernatural covering over every part of you that leads to your heart causing it to be infiltrated. May the Lord place a guard over your ears, eyes, mouth, mind and emotions bringing you into full stability and good health. In Jesus name, Amen.

Day 153

Bitter Roots

The peace and the love of God cares about us so much that He won't leave us the same (Romans 5:8). He is able to search our hearts, reveal what's in our hearts to us and then give us the assurance of His love that He will see us through to remove what doesn't belong. We don't have to be alone when it comes to the matters of the heart with God. He has a way of showing us that He is the safest place for our heart to begin its process of healing (Psalm 147:3).

As you make that intentional prayer and intimacy time with God, prepare for your heart to have that warm feeling again. That warm feeling that brings us back home. God wants to give us children peace about the security of our hearts in Him.

Let downs, frustration, disappointments will happen but as God grows you stronger He will bless you to respond differently. Your response will no longer leave you with the poison from bitter roots growing causing vines with thorns around your heart (See this in a spiritual sense) to grow bitter and bitter as your heart turns into stone (Ezekiel 36:26).

Bitterness can lead to vengeance, hate, and a mean spirit. Those in need of healing by the matters of your heart, I feel the Lord making it clear that He sees our heart with the stings of life's disappointments. God still has a plan to bring you to an expected end (Jeremiah 29:11).

Day 154

Grace Beyond Measure

There is grace in your brokenness. But to each of us has been given grace according to the measure of the gift of the Christ (Ephesians 4:7). God knows everything it takes to break you, but He also knows how to make you and build you back up because the truth is we need to be made over in our hearts and minds every day. We have to pray over ourselves that bitterness would not spread in us (Hebrews 12:15).

Hurt can cause us to recognize a person in us we don't even know. Because you have been disappointed it can cause you to draw back from everything and build a wall up keeping anyone from coming close to you again. Make sure there is no man or woman, clan or tribe among you today whose heart turns away from the Lord our God to go and worship the gods of those nations; make sure there is no root among you that produces such bitter poison (Deuteronomy 29:18).

For the eyes of the Lord range throughout the earth to strengthen those whose hearts are fully committed to Him (2 Chronicles 16:9).

Day 155

Under Pressure

Through the chaos or mishaps of the world have we allowed the Holy Spirit to guide us to the heart of the Father? We have to be able to resist and fight the urges of our flesh whenever uncontrollable circumstances are unraveling around us. When we are under pressure it seems like everything in us starts to rise up that would cause us to go backwards. Old desires may try to arise on how we used to handle our stress but there is a call deep down on the inside of our bellies waiting for the Holy Spirit to fall fresh in us.

When the Holy Spirit falls fresh then new songs of deliverance can come forth. You may even find that the song may be a familiar sound but that your voice is different, the works of your heart start to respond differently to what the Lord has done based on where He has brought you from.

As you develop consistency in your devotion time with God you will see that your heart is becoming more courageous, and you have the capability to patiently wait on God (Psalm 27:14).

When your conscience is clear you are able to keep your mind in heavenly places (Ephesians 1:3). God wants to teach his people how to keep our mind in heavenly places even if the outside world is chaotic. We are responsible for what flows on the inside of us.

Prayer: "Lord help me not to be easily angered or offended. Help me not to get upset with circumstances that would plague my mind keeping my conscience from being clear in You. In Jesus name I pray, Amen.

Day 156
Safe Place

We are alive by the goodness of God. God's goodness is a promise to us from His Word, but we have to dwell and settle in with God. "Surely goodness and mercy shall follow me all the days of my life; and I will dwell in the house of the Lord forever" (Psalm 23:6). Stay locked in with God because His Presence is the safest place we can ever be in.

God's goodness brings comfort yet correction when needed. There is so much comfort in knowing we serve a God who sees the best of us and knows how to bring us to be our best selves as time goes on. He disciplines us with love yet encourages us that it is for the better.

"The Lord is a safe place for the oppressed, a safe place in difficult times. Those who know your name trust you because you have not abandoned any who seek you, Lord." (Psalms 9:9-10)

Day 157
Come Alive

At the breath of God your mind, body and spirit will respond. God is calling you to come up out of the low and dry places in spite of how you feel, good things are getting ready to happen! The wind from God's breath is bringing order to our emotions and setting us forth to prosper with a good attitude. When God teaches you to focus on His goodness it leaves no room for a bad attitude or dwelling in the past.

The Lord is personally teaching me to remain focused, so my mood won't be thrown off and out of order. The Spirit of God is what's going to renew and rebuild you bringing forth stability from the inside out. For God has not given us a spirit of fear and timidity, but of power, love, self-discipline, self-control, sound judgment and a sound mind (2 Timothy 1:7).

Thus says the Lord God to these bones, 'Behold, I will cause breath to enter you that you may come to life. I will put sinews on you, make flesh grow back on you, cover you with skin and put breath in you that you may come alive; and you will know that I am the Lord.'". (Ezekiel 37:5-6)

Day 158
God Meets Us More Than Halfway

The Lord placed a word on my heart about learning to release and allowing Him to guide us as we give our cares to Him. No matter how you feel, acknowledge God, even when your emotions and mind are in a place that's not so good. To be in constant fear, worry, and anxiety is not the way Abba has created us to live. When you lay what's burdening you down, letting your worries go and refusing to not pick them back up, pick the Word of God and meditate on Scriptures designed for your specific circumstance.

No matter where you find yourself, God wants you to come to Him as your Heavenly Father. With trust and security, along with peace, knowing you will be heard and guided along the right path (Proverbs 3:5-6). When we pray, it can feel like God is someone who is far away, but His presence is all around us, and His Spirit is in us by the renewal and baptizing of the Holy Spirit (Acts 2:38-39).

As we continue to practice God's word more regularly, we gain strength, wisdom, understanding, knowledge, direction, and assurance. Then we are able to get His word down on our spirit, so when trouble does come, we don't have to feel like we are constantly forcing our mind to believe what should already be in our spirit man. We have to get mature enough in our faith to let our challenges teach us to run to God, not run from God. Besides, apart from Him we can't do anything. We need Him just to breathe because He is the One who provides the air in our lungs.

"1 I bless God every chance I get; my lungs expand with his praise. 2 I live and breathe God; if things aren't going well, hear this and be happy: 3 Join me in spreading the news; together let's get the word out. 4 God met me more than halfway, he freed me from my anxious fears. 5 Look at him; give him your warmest smile. Never hide your feelings from him. 6 When I was desperate, I called out, and God got me out of a tight spot.

7 God's angel sets up a circle of protection around us while we pray. 8 Open your mouth and taste, open your eyes and see— how good God is. Blessed are you who run to him. 9 Worship God if you want the best; worship opens doors to all his goodness. 10 Young lions on the prowl get hungry, but God-seekers are full of God. 11 Come, children, listen closely; I'll give you a lesson in God worship. 12 Who out there has a lust for life? Can't wait each day to come upon beauty?

13 Guard your tongue from profanity, and no more lying through your teeth. 14 Turn your back on sin; do something good. Embrace peace—don't let it get away! 15 God keeps an eye on his friends, his ears pick up every moan and groan. 16 God won't put up with rebels; he'll cull them from the pack. 17 Is anyone crying for help? God is listening, ready to rescue you. 18 If your heart is broken, you'll find God right there; if you're kicked in the gut, he'll help you catch your breath."
(Psalms 34:1-18 MSG)

Day 159

Awaits You

Let God make your rough places smooth (Isaiah 45:2). Remember, the Lord desires for us to come to Him in all things, no matter how good or bad we are feeling. Just when you feel like giving up, God steps in and shows you that He can turn your worst days into the best days of your life.

Even in your weaknesses, you can still be made strong through the power of Christ that shall rest on you as you let Him in (2 Corinthians 12:9). God desires to come in and rest in the walls of your heart. No matter what you may have to face today, when things start to get overwhelming, lay your hand on your heart and be present of what you feel.

As you practice mindfulness and feel your heart beating, remember that there is still life in you, and that all is not lost. Your heartbeat signifies that there is purpose and destiny that awaits you.

"What blessings await you when people hate you and exclude you and mock you and curse you as evil because you follow the Son of Man. When that happens, be happy! Yes, leap for joy! For a great reward awaits you in heaven. And remember, their ancestors treated the ancient prophets that same way." (Luke 6:22-23)

Scripture Luke 6:27-38:

"But to you who are willing to listen, I say, love your enemies! Do good to those who hate you. Bless those who curse you. Pray for those who hurt you. If someone slaps you on one cheek, offer the other cheek also. If someone demands your coat, offer your shirt also. Give to anyone

who asks; and when things are taken away from you, don't try to get them back. Do to others as you would like them to do to you. "If you love only those who love you, why should you get credit for that?

Even sinners love those who love them! And if you do good only to those who do good to you, why should you get credit? Even sinners do that much! And if you lend money only to those who can repay you, why should you get credit? Even sinners will lend to other sinners for a full return. "Love your enemies! Do good to them. Lend to them without expecting to be repaid. Then your reward from heaven will be very great, and you will truly be acting as children of the Most High, for he is kind to those who are unthankful and wicked. You must be compassionate, just as your Father is compassionate.

"Do not judge others, and you will not be judged. Do not condemn others, or it will all come back against you. Forgive others, and you will be forgiven. Give, and you will receive. Your gift will return to you in full, pressed down, shaken together to make room for more, running over, and poured into your lap. The amount you give will determine the amount you get back." In the name of Jesus, Amen.

Day 160

Keep Going

Sometimes others won't always see your growth but that doesn't mean that you should stop trying. As long as you know and most of all God knows then that's all that matters. You are more than just a person with potential, you are a person with purpose. Only for a moment our emotions, afflictions and troubles are temporary.

Sometimes it's going to feel like the more steps you take the more life tries to knock you down, keep going! You may make mistakes more than you would like, keep going! don't let your breakdowns convince you that breakthrough is not near. We can all continue to grow knowing that we are forgiven, as we confess and give our shortcomings to the Lord, allowing Him to come in and work through us to be better.

You may feel overlooked by those around you but just believe and know, God sees you and knows when to call your name encouraging you to come forth. Keep your head up, don't keep crying over to the "thing" that God wants to give you rest from. Don't be afraid of what it is you will have to overcome in this journey, it may be new to you but it's not new to God. He has the solution.

Scripture references: 2 Corinthians 4:17, Colossians 2:14, Jeremiah 29:11

Day 161

Ransom For Many

Be encouraged and strengthened this morning by not doubting one second of your life. What doesn't make sense now will be more clear later. What God allowed you to live through, He will use that same circumstance for you to minister to someone else and encourage them that if they just believe and hold on that they will see the goodness of the Lord. What you didn't die in God can use you to help someone live through their situation as an overcomer.

"Be like the Son of Man. He did not come to be served. Instead, he came to serve others. He came to give his life as the price for setting many people free." (Matthew 20:28)

Your current struggle will not be your forever struggle. Clouds have to form in our lives for the rain to come forth. This is a broken and fallen world. We want the sunshine, but we forget that we also have to learn to appreciate and walk through the cloudy and rainy days. We can still look to the Author and Finisher of our faith (Hebrews 12:2), calling on His name whether we are in the sun or the rain.

Our faith is built in the good and the "bad" days. Your struggles and success teaches you who to take refuge in, being that Jesus is constant and solid whether you are up or down. He won't leave you when things get tough and when you're down to your last like how people can do. Jesus is our solid rock (Psalm 18:2).

Day 162
God's Specialty

God specializes in transforming lives. He has the ability to turn the impossible into the possible. He has the capability to turn trials into blessings. The God who wipes away tears, who provides the cloud by day and fire by night. There is comfort in knowing God is always with us.

This is a new day filled with new mercies. In spite of how you feel, don't rob yourself of seeing the beauty that lies in this day, even if you are used to experiencing the same things throughout your day from previous days. We can't let what was set our tone for the new day that's here now. God desires for us to be free from the captivity of our own thoughts.

When we lean into our own understanding, we can get lost there because we don't see the full picture like God does. When we make room for God, He can come in and deliver us from anything that is causing us to be bound. This encouraging message for today is to lift us up, knowing we can come out of our low places and live! We shall overcome by the blood of the lamb and the words of our testimony.

Scripture references: Revelation 21:4, Matthew 19:26, Exodus 13:21-22, Lamentations 3:22-23, Revelation 12:11

Prayer: God, I am expecting something big to happen today, give me the discernment and wisdom to know that You are near. Thank You for all that you have in store for me. Don't let the trouble that lies in the day blind me from seeing the treasure you have stored for me on this day. Heavenly

Father, take hold of my thoughts so I can think better. Lord, remove the spirit of overthinking and replaying my hurt and what was over and over in my head. You are my Shepherd, and I shall not want (Psalm 23:1). In Jesus name, Amen.

Day 163
Seedtime and Harvest

When you feel like you are just here, going through the motions of life barely making it, remember that God is always in motion, moving and working behind the scenes for your life, aligning things to come into place for you. God is well aware and knows every detail of our lives and situations. Our encouragement for today is that we have a promise to hold on to in the middle of our struggles. The promise is,

"God is not man, that he should lie, or a son of man, that he should change his mind or repent. Has he said, and will he not do it? Or has he spoken, and will he not fulfill it?" (*Numbers 23:19 ESV*).

Only God can do it, whatever your "it" is. Thank God for your "it." It may not feel good; it may be crushing and paining you, but your "it" is teaching you just how real God is and how great He is by His ability to overthrow the impossibilities. Which means your life has to evolve in pursuit of what God has said.

When we think about the word evolve, it means to change over time. You may be facing the worst battle of your life right now, but it's temporary, it has to change, even if it means it will take some time. Sometimes life has to bring you to your knees so that the Lord can teach you how to pray and then stand.

Prayer: Heavenly Father, bless me with a spirit that doesn't mind waiting on you. God grant my heart the strength that your word will fall on good ground that I would receive 100-fold (Luke 8:8). Give me the supernatural strength to believe that I will be strong enough to resist the enemy's attempts to steal what you planted in me. Be rooted in me. Lord, keep my heart from being rocky soil (Luke 8:6-7). Help me to not live my life wasting the potential you have placed in me to fulfill the purpose you have for my life. Let my character be of good fruit from your tree, by the birthing of the Holy Spirit. In Jesus name, Amen.

Day 164

Between a Rock

This is an appreciation devotional for those who push through and show up, even when it comes to showing up to your hard places. Whatever your "hard place" is, if no one else hasn't told you, I just want to say, "Thank you, and you are appreciated. Thank you for all that you do, even when it feels like you want to walk out because you feel stuck between a rock and your hard place."

It's easy to feel unseen and unappreciated when things are hard. After many long days at work, I have had to tell myself, "Thank you for showing up and all that you have given on this day. You may not have accomplished everything and weren't able to meet the needs of everyone, but you can be at peace knowing you have done the best with what you were given and required to do."

Outside of our hard places, we still have to show up for our passion, purpose, loved ones, ministry, or whatever it is the Lord has your hands to do. The key principle to remember is that any of these will not be possible or healthy to function in if we don't learn how to properly love and take care of ourselves in order to be available to anyone or anything else.

Prayer: Isaiah 40:31, "Lord, help me to wait on You so that my strength can be renewed. Bless me to mount up with wings like an eagle and soar through my hard places. I am expecting to receive from Your Holy Spirit, the strength to run and not grow weary, and the courage to walk and not faint. Remove any guilt and guard me from any backlash for standing up for myself and learning to put me first for a chance." In Jesus name, I pray, Amen.

Day 165

It Won't Work

Scripture and encouragement is coming from Isaiah 54:17. No matter what's forming up against you, it will not prosper. People can speak against you, but it won't stop God from speaking for you and over you. Life is not over yet for me because I shall live and not die and declare the works of the Lord (Psalm 118:17). It's so encouraging to know that God can keep His people in what the enemy expected you to die in. You may have been feeling down, but you won't die there! The events of life may have tried to discourage me from continuing to encourage God's people, but it ain't over until God says it's over.

Prayer: Heavenly Father, shape my heart and mind with strength. Pour Your oil on me so that I can be a glory carrier. Help me to not lean on my own understanding and to trust You through the process of bringing out the product You want to bring out of this current trial. Let Your love grow in me stronger than hate, strife, vengeance, and unforgiveness would. Help me to be thankful and humble about my trials. I know that Your word tells me in Romans 8:28 that all things work together for the good of those who love You, God, and are called according to Your purpose. Grant me supernatural peace through this trial.

Keep my tongue humble to only speak Your word, that is the living truth (John 17:17). Forgive me when I fall short of Your glory and when I choose not to operate out of a spirit of maturity, wisdom, and love. Continue to create in me a new mind and heart that will be able to walk out of this thing called life. In the midst of adversity, help me to remember that no matter what it feels like, I have goodness and mercy following me (Psalm 23:6).

Build my spirit up so that I won't be torn down by the words of other people but that I will use the Word of God as my weapon. Help me to be unrecognizable by the power of Your word. Lord, give me the strength to stay in a place higher than what the enemy wouldn't be able to go up to. Your way is higher and better, Lord (Isaiah 55:9). No matter what others may think about me, I know Your thoughts are good towards me (Jeremiah 29:11). I can walk in confidence, knowing Your love and forgiveness are what's holding me up. People may come and go, but I'm so glad that You, Lord, will remain with me forever (Deuteronomy 31:8).

Thank You for fighting every battle (Exodus 14:14) and giving me the grace to take my hands off of what you are planning to bring correction to. I will not settle in discouragement in the name of Jesus. I don't have to get comfortable in weariness whenever You are my resting place (Psalm 91:1). Give me an overflow of healing thoughts so I can keep my mind focused on Your will. In Jesus name, Amen.

Day 166

Present Your Requests

If your situation isn't good yet, then God is not finished yet. Whatever it is that you're going through, there can still be a mighty turnaround attached to your story. While we are believing by faith for things to turn around, we have to pray over ourselves that our hearts will make a joyful noise continuously. Sometimes life can get us so down that our hearts hurt so loud from life's disappointments, setbacks, and inconveniences that our praise can be threatened if we let it. The attacks and opposition in your life can either mute you or make you.

I find myself making a declaration whenever that spirit of depression, confusion, and anxiety tries to hit. "I will make a joyful noise unto the Lord no matter what I'm going through." Certain situations and people may be frustrating, but Lord, let my heart cry out for you just as the rocks would (Luke 19:40). Nothing should be able to take our praise, even though sometimes it feels like it's easier said than done. This message is to empower you to not lose your voice and praise. Let your sound of praise be louder than your sound of sorrow. Do not be anxious about anything, but in every situation, by prayer and petition, with thanksgiving, present your requests to God (Philippians 4:6).

Prayer: Heavenly Father, bless me to hold on to see the evidence of my faith. Your word tells me, Now faith is the substance of things hoped for, the evidence of things not seen (Hebrews 11:1). Help me to hold on to You so that I can obtain a good testimony. Whenever I am feeling weary, Lord, give me renewed eyes of faith. I may not be able to see the full picture, but settle my spirit to trust in the way of You, Lord. Lift me higher so that I will not let anything come and stand in the middle of me calling on Your Name, Jesus. Thank you for training my hands for war and my fingers for battle (Psalm 144:1). In Jesus name, Amen.

Day 167
God's Incomparable Great Power

You may find yourself with the same need waiting to be met. Prayers that have yet to come to pass, but you are still believing God for what you need. I'm praying that each of us will be able to see with our hearts what our eyes can't see.

Ephesians 1:17-21, "I keep asking that the God of our Lord Jesus Christ, the glorious Father, may give each of us the Spirit of wisdom and revelation, so that we may know him better. I pray that the eyes of our hearts may be enlightened in order that we may know the hope to which he has called us, the riches of his glorious inheritance in his holy people, and his incomparably great power for us who believe. That power is the same as the mighty strength he exerted when he raised Christ from the dead and seated him at his right hand in the heavenly realms, far above all rule and authority, power and dominion, and every name that is invoked, not only in the present age but also in the one to come." (NIV)

God has all power in His hands; He doesn't have some or a little, but all power. Even in the midst of our needs, God already has an answer (Psalm 91:15). Truly, sometimes we don't even know what we need. We can become impatient because we want everything to work out according to our own timing. Be encouraged on this day, knowing God's timing is always perfect.

"But do not forget this one thing, dear friends: With the Lord a day is like a thousand years, and a thousand years are like a day. The Lord is not slow in keeping his promise,

as some understand slowness (2 Peter 3:8-9)."

God goes ahead of us (Deuteronomy 31:8). Even in situations that look bad, there is still some good we can pull out of it. Your night season won't last forever, because greater is He that's in you than He that's in the world (1 John 4:4). Our rest in hard times begins when we remember His grace and mercy that have been with us and our remembrance of the last time He made a way.

It's important to be around people who are going to believe in God with you and for you. It's bad enough that our own thoughts try to come against us and make us doubt. There can be people who see and are aware of what you stand in need of and say, "You may as well give up because it ain't happening." Taking on someone else's doubt and unbelief won't make things better either. This is a time when our atmosphere needs to be set with faith, belief, and hope. Because God can bless you at any time and any place.

Day 168
My Soul Says Yes

Life is filled with uncertainties, but that does not mean God is unsure or uncertain about you. We can rest assured and be certain that God knows us by name (Exodus 33:17) and knows our story from the beginning to the end (Psalm 139).

"My sheep hear my voice, and I know them, and they follow me: and I give unto them eternal life; and they shall never perish, neither shall any man pluck them out of my hand (John 10:27-28 KJV)".

This scripture is so encouraging to know that we are secured and locked in with God. As much as we dread that a certain situation doesn't always change immediately for us, the truth is, time is a form of protection because we wouldn't be able to handle all of life's uncertainties at one time. Even when facing uncertainties, we have to learn to develop unwavering faith and trust in God.

Even when you are in the fire, don't lose your fire for God. Our fire for God is preserved when we learn how to be faithful to Him no matter the circumstance and when we yield to the Holy Spirit and give Him an honest yes. "Here I am, send me! (Isaiah 6:8)." God honors the words of our heart. They mean more than the words that're coming out of a mouth whose heart is far from what the mouth speaks.

Day 169

Be Gracious to Me

God's got a plan for you. Thank Him for the tears. Let this day be filled with thanksgiving. Yes, your current pain and hurt may seem to run deep, but take comfort in His love that endures forever (Psalm 106:1). Your tears don't have to be in vain when God has the ability to use the same thing you cried over to cause you to be an overcomer. Your tears don't take away from the fact that your name is already written on the blessings coming your way.

Remember, failure is part of succeeding. You have to know what it's like to fail and then learn from your mistakes in order to be successful. We have to learn to serve the Lord with all humility, with tears, and with trials that can come upon us through the plots of our enemies (Acts 20:19). When you are down and out, especially at night because that's the time when you are laying down and your thoughts race the most, speak over yourself and say, "Lord, I trust that there is a miracle attached to every tear."

"Have mercy on me, O Lord, for I am in trouble; My eye wastes away with grief, Yes, my soul and my body!" NKJV(Psalms 31:9)

Day 170

Whispers of the Heart

Discouragement doesn't have to become a place of settlement for us. God reigns over our discouragement and let downs. The only answer to our problems that are bigger than us is to call on a God who is bigger than our problems. When the unexpected hits, we should seek the Lord and expect Him to answer in His own way and timing (Ecclesiastes 3:1).

The weight on your back is getting ready to be lifted by the wind of God. The wind of God is going to blow a supernatural strength on you that will give you rest for your current season. This strength is going to cause you to see the night from day. Because when you have been in a season of weariness for so long, it's hard to tell the difference between the two. God hears the whispers of our hearts. This encounter with the Lord is going to give you a spirit of endurance. Just as sure as the sun rises and sets by the order of God, our lives have to be formed and set by the demand and Word of God over our lives.

Prayer: Heavenly Father, Thank You for the gift of life You have given me today. I am alive and kept by Your grace. I was able to move and have my being without any hurt, harm, or endangerment. Thank You for allowing me to get in my car and drive from place to place accident free.

Now, God, I am coming to You so that I can give you my mind and ask You to help me with constant overthinking. When life's interruptions come, help me to respond in the way Heaven expects me to respond. I know that life is not only what happens to us but also how we respond. Give me a renewed strength that will cause me to respond to situations like a child of the Most High King. In Jesus name, I pray, Amen.

Day 171
Abundance

The first way to activate abundance is through the mind. We often think abundance starts with monetary or materialistic things, but it starts in the mind and our soul first. Abundance from God is a lifetime harvest. As our minds and hearts are renewed daily, we grow in abundance. Abundance starts with peace, rest, assurance of your identity, forgiveness, humility, and love, to name a few.

We are God's handiwork, created in Christ Jesus to do good works, which God prepared in advance for us to do. The harvest of abundance does have enemies known as harvest thieves, who come only to steal, kill, and destroy. Jesus came so that we may have life more abundantly. Every form of sorrow has to turn into joy. Sorrow and grief is temporary, but the joy that Jesus gives us is eternal.

In the midst of cultivating an abundance mindset, we will go through tests and situations that are going to make us feel like we are not strong enough to take on what comes our way. The truth is that the bad news we receive at first sometimes seems realer than the good news coming to pass—that things will get better. But there is a promise we can hold on to—that when it's all said and done, God makes all things good in His timing.

Scripture references: Ephesians 2:10; John 10:10; John 16:20; John 16:22; Romans 8:28

Day 172
Intentionality of God

This inspirational devotion of encouragement is based on the intentionality of God. God is so intentional about us that when we were once far off from Him, He already had us drawn close to His heart to provide freedom and salvation for us. Even when we didn't realize we needed it. God clearly shows and proves His own love for us by the fact that, while we were still sinners, Christ died for us.

Before we shift into another place with God, we have to level up on our intentionality towards God. Be willing to seek Him above all else. As you seek God, everything else you need will come. Your intentionality for God can be measured by what you do on a daily basis. This is a sensitive time. If you are not committed to God, I feel the Lord is encouraging many to get committed to Him, and if you are committed to Him, stay committed like never before. Now is not the time to drift away because you may be experiencing some fire or in deep water.

Find out the likes and dislikes of God, what honors and dishonors Him, and live according to what He approves and expects of those who are His people. We have to try our best to be intentional and not do what is dishonorable to God and break His heart. Give God all of you, especially the broken parts of you. The broken parts of us are what God uses to bring us breakthroughs. The broken parts shift us to be humble and teachable. The sacrifices of a broken spirit and a broken and contrite heart God will not despise.

That way, when it's all said and done, He will get the glory, and it will be clear that only God was the One who made a way for you. All the unnecessary parts and ways of you will fall off when you make God necessary in your life. The church encourages us to come as we are, but God does not encourage us to stay as we are.

As you intentionally position yourself to be in God's presence, yield to what He wants to remove from you, and open yourself up to what He wants to put in you as a new creation in Christ Jesus, then you can see that the Holy Spirit is capable of doing the work in you.

"Therefore if any man be in Christ, he is a new creature: old things have passed away; behold, all things have become new." (2 Corinthians 5:17)

Scripture references: Matthew 6:33; Romans 5:8; Psalm 51:17

Day 173
Spiritual Minded

No matter how hard life hits don't stop believing God for your miracle. God has been and still is revealing Himself as the Great I Am. In this upcoming life changing encounter with God, He is reassuring His people of what it means for Him to be I Am and what it means for you to have the Great I Am on the inside of you. The power in biblical affirmations is what causes you to go over and above in victory as you are experiencing afflictions that would normally cause people to go under. As you continue to take purpose filled steps towards bettering yourself and walking in positivity, remember to take time to uplift and encourage yourself throughout the day. It's a million things that can happen throughout the day to alter your mood. But the million things that can happen throughout the day won't stop the move of God, because He is a wheel in the middle of a wheel.

God's mobility is not limited. God can work around any situation. Nothing is too hard or hidden from Him. Jesus is our greatest burden-bearer. Burden bearers see your need underneath the surface-level need. Don't block yourself from connecting with God, who is in you, based on how you feel and what you're going through. Your carnal mind can keep you disconnected from your spiritual mind, if you don't learn how to discipline yourself to choose God over yourself and how you feel. The spiritual goal of believers should be to walk by the Spirit at all times. To be carnal minded is death, and to be spiritual minded is life and peace.

Scripture references: Exodus 3:14; Ezekiel 1:16; 10:10; Psalm 55:22; 1 John 4:4; Romans 8:6

Day 174

Love Covers

In the midst of suffering, God has a way of allowing us to experience His goodness and His love. His love covers a multitude of sins. Therefore, we have to love and forgive others just as Christ does for us daily. Even in your suffering, it is essential for us to learn how to keep pushing, pray, and praise. God dwells where there is praise. God inhabits the praises of His people. Our praise is what will break the yokes and tear down the strongholds. He will destroy the yokes while you are praising Him. He will tear down the strongholds while you are praising Him. When you shift your focus to the Lord, it makes room for Him to come in as the King of Glory and Lord of Hope, to where the heavy burdens have to come out and be lifted off of you.

For those who feel like they have been captive and bound, the Lord says, "Come out," and for those who feel like they have been in darkness, the Lord says, "Be free!." You may feel like you've been down and out, but the Lord says, "I am the Lord your God, who teaches you what is best for you, who directs you in the way you should go." You may feel like you have nothing or no one, but there is still hope for you. The Earth is the Lord's, and everything in it, the world, and all who live on it. God can turn our nothing into something because He loves us unconditionally.

Scripture references: 1 Peter 4:8; Psalm 22:3; Isaiah 49:9; Isaiah 48:18; Psalm 24:1-2

Day 175

Stirred For More

God's word gives us a new beginning. God's word teaches us the breadth and depth of true life, so we won't remain in continuous torment by sin. God not only encourages us but also corrects us when we are out of alignment with Him. We all have tendencies that we need deliverance from. We become saved, but the truth is that the ways and habits we adapted to before we got saved call for a mighty deliverance.

"Those who consider themselves religious and yet do not keep a tight rein on their tongues deceive themselves, and their religion is worthless (James 1:26)."

Give God every thought, word, and action you have made, and leave them with Him. When we intentionally commit ourselves to God, then our feet will stay on the path where living waters flow. Old ways won't produce new growth. When you are not growing, you are blocking yourself from new doors opening. The more time we spend in God's presence, the greater the stir in us should be to grow into who He has called us to be. The Holy Spirit has to be in full control so that God can prepare you for what He wants to do in your life. God's word is a lifestyle and food for the souls of believers. Keeping watch over your tongue is like keeping watch over your soul.

Prayer: Heavenly Father, let my thoughts, words, actions be integrity filled. Bless me to be disciplined and self-controlled as I go on my day-to-day walk. Help me to see and believe that I can do all things through Christ who strengthens me (Philippians 4:13).

Forgive me for the ways and habits that I have clung to over the years. Thank you for giving me a humble and still spirit that I would allow You to fight my battles. Lord, bless me with a more faithful and obedient spirit to do Your will. In Jesus name, Amen.

Day 176

Strength of My Heart

Our flesh and heart will fail us but even when we feel like we are failing, God already has a way and plan for us to bounce back from every setback.

"My health may fail, and my spirit may grow weak, but God remains the strength of my heart; he is mine forever (Psalms 73:2 NLT)."

You may feel like you are at the end of the road, maybe your emotions have led you to a place that you thought you could never return from. There is always a word from the Bible that was made specifically for whatever it is that's currently worrying you, being that there is nothing new under the sun (Ecclesiastes 1:9). If you hold on, stand firm in your faith, and trust God He will get the glory out of whatever is worrying you.

Prayer: Heavenly Father, Thank You for this new day. Thank You for never giving up on me. Even when I mess up, the strength of Your unconditional love draws me back into Your Arms. Lord, help me to see the sunshine from within me even when my sight seems to be gloomy, making everything gray around me. Thank you for restoring my strength so that I am able to walk in a manner worthy of the calling to which I have been called to by You (Ephesians 4:1). In Jesus name I pray, Amen.

Day 177
Place of Worship

God desires to be the focus point of our lives. Today's encouraging devotion comes from Acts 16:16-40. You may have been feeling like life has been beating you down to the point where you view yourself as completely broken. What we see as brokenness in a bad sense, God sees it as His way of breaking new ground in us for His goodness to be revealed. Don't lose your praise in the midst of what you are going through, because others will be set free on the account of your prayer and praise.

Territories and opportunities that were once closed off from you have to open up as your voice reaches heaven. After Paul and Silas were stripped and beaten until they were black and blue, followed by being thrown in prison. They still had praise on the inside. The persecution they were under didn't stop them from praying and singing hymns unto the Lord. If you are wondering where your joy is in the eye of your storm, it's in His presence.

If you are wondering where your peace is when everything around you looks distorted, it's in His presence. If you are wondering where your freedom is after you have found yourself in repeated cycles that have held you up to where you were bound and captive, it's in His presence. The praises of God's people can make the earth shake! Even though you may be suffering, there is someone who is listening out for the voice God has placed on the inside of you. Every gift that God has placed in your innermost being will be a blessing to help set others free in the name of Jesus.

Day 178
Right Hand of God

Pay attention to how people you think are good for you treat you when others are around. It's like they care for you in private, but in public they don't recognize you. It's time out for allowing people to treat you like an option while you prioritize them. Watch out for those who will tolerate you for their own benefit, even though they can't stand you. When the enemy uses people and they start playing dirty, you have to change your territory.

The serpent knows how to blend in, this is why it's so important to be aware of the company you keep. Everyone around you does not want to see you blessed. God is the God of turnaround. Pray for sharper discernment and to know what to do with what God reveals to you. God knows who is counterfeit in your life, so that's why it's important to trust God in what He shows you.

Don't try to force others to see or understand you. We have to learn to stop trying to show people who we are and let God Himself show who we are. We have to let God's word over our lives speak for us. Sometimes people's agenda and God's agenda are different. God knows how to announce you at the right time. Keep being you, and don't change who God is calling you to be for anyone.

"For it is God's will that by doing good you should silence the ignorant talk of foolish people." (1 Peter 2:15)

God will put your enemies under your feet. This devotion is to bring us focus, stir our memory of who God is, and remind us of His right hand of goodness. We often, in prayer, tell God about our situations more often than we take the time to tell our situations about our God. We have to learn to take the time to strengthen our faith and not worry about what we can't control.

God is our help in hardship. His Word is our daily bread for our everyday battles. God is our hope in a hopeless world. Jesus is our peace in chaos. Jesus is our calm in the eye of the storm. He is our faith that keeps us from failing. We have to learn how to sit at the right hand of God and let Him make our enemies who oppose us our footstool.

The benefits of God's right hand is that we experience His hand of strength, we experience pleasures forevermore, He holds us up, and His right hand is full of righteousness. The right hand of the Lord has planted the root that became our salvation. He keeps you next to Him by holding onto your right hand. God's right hand makes us immovable.

Scripture references: Matthew 22:44; Exodus 15:6; Psalms 16:11; Psalms 18:35; Psalm 48:10; Psalm 80:14-15; Psalm 73:23; Psalm 16:8

Serenity Prayer: "God, grant me the serenity to accept the things I cannot change. The courage to change the things I can and the wisdom to know the difference. Living one day at a time. Enjoying one moment at a time. Accepting hardships as the pathway to peace. Taking, as Jesus did, this sinful world as it is, not as I would have it. Trusting that You will make things right if I surrender to Your will, so that I may be reasonably happy in this life and supremely happy with You forever and ever in the next. In Jesus name, I pray, Amen."

Day 179

Bless My Plans Lord

God always has a plan to overturn and supersede the enemy's plots. God's people can take comfort in the fact that He has the last and final say. Whatever is standing in the way of your peace, growth, success, health, mind, joy, your salvation, and most of all the will of God for your life, has a set time ordained by God Himself to come to an end. Those things sent to cause confusion, frustration, disorder, separation, chaos, delay, and distraction will be uprooted and destroyed on the account of what God has purposed for His people's lives.

"We may make our plans, but God has the last word. You may think everything you do is right, but the Lord judges your motives. Ask the Lord to bless your plans, and you will be successful in carrying them out. Everything the Lord has made has its destiny; and the destiny of the wicked is destruction. The Lord hates everyone who is arrogant; he will never let them escape punishment. Be loyal and faithful, and God will forgive your sin. Obey the Lord and nothing evil will happen to you. When you please the Lord, you can make your enemies into friends. It is better to have a little, honestly earned, than to have a large income gained dishonestly. You may make your plans, but God directs your actions." (Proverbs 16:1-9 GNBUK: Good News Bible (British Version) 2017)

Day 180

In Due Season

Just because things haven't come to pass yet, it doesn't mean it won't come at all.

"And let us not be weary in well doing: for in due season we shall reap, if we faint not." (Galatians 6:9)

In this next move of God He will make all things beautiful. He will make whatever you need last. We don't have to stress, worry, or cry over what is ordained to come into our lives in God's timing. We may not always know when, where or who but it is all in His divine will and plan for us to prosper.

"Beloved, I wish above all things that you may prosper and be in health, even as your soul prospers." (3 John 1:2)

God wants to get our soul right before we get the blessings He has for us. He can bless us, but we have to pray for wisdom and patience to receive and learn how to not misuse what God gives us. Give thanks unto the Lord first and then expect to see multiplication with what is in your hands (John 6:11).

Even though we want things to happen our way and on our time, the truth is it doesn't happen that way. God is in control, and we have to learn to humble ourselves and trust that God knows when to bring what we need to pass. Remember it's a time and season for all things (Ecclesiastes 3:1).

Prayer: Heavenly Father, bless me with a patient spirit to allow You to work things out in my favor. Forgive me for when I didn't realize that I wasn't fully trusting You. Reset my eyes on You. Grant me with the necessary courage and confidence to be obedient unto You. Help me to not stress over the WHEN but put my trust and energy into worshiping You. Thank You Lord, Amen.

Day 181

Keep the Vision

Don't be so busy complaining that you miss God when He answers your prayers. Sometimes God allows inconveniences to lighten our load and for God to intervene. Inconveniences show us what's in us. Don't miss the moments you have been waiting so long for. He didn't tell us to complain, but to be watchful and prayerful (Colossians 4:2).

"Rejoice always, pray without ceasing, give thanks in all circumstances; for this is the will of God in Christ Jesus for you (1 Thessalonians 5:16-18)".

Whenever we wait on God He blesses us with more than what we expected. Instead of a complaining spirit we have to pray over ourselves that the Lord would give us a spirit that compliments who He is as the King of kings and Lord of lords. Complaining can cut off your vision for what God has promised you, causing you to believe that better is not coming.

"The vision of the evenings and mornings that has been given you is true, but seal up the vision, for it concerns the distant future." (Daniel 8:26)

God does the justice of pulling us out of low places and then when we get to the next place, we complain. We have to pray that our complaining won't destroy us. In the Old Testament while being in the wilderness transitioning into the promised land God's people had complaining spirits even after the Lord had provided and gave them victory after being delivered out of Pharaoh's hand. Don't go back to those old places that no longer serve you because you don't see how God will provide for you in the new places He is calling you to. Though easier said than done, the chaos around us shouldn't lead us to complain but whenever chaos is present we should be led to pray.

Day 182

Behold

The way God has prepared for you is already prepared. It's just about walking in divine timing to the destination He wants to bring you to. When the constant worry and the what-if's come, speak to your situation, and announce to the enemy that God will bring me up and over. God wants to bring us out with a new mind in Him. Each of us has different stories that may be filled with more of the unimaginable than others, but we can all testify and say that it is the life and favor of Jesus Christ that has brought us through.

With God, we don't have to manipulate situations for outcomes to turn in our favor. If God has called something to be so in our lives, then it will be so. No matter the storm, how strong the winds are, or how heavy the rain is, God has sovereignty over everything! We have to learn how to stop giving our energy to battles sent to drain and tire us out when God simply just wants us to pray and give thanks for the outcome He has coming to work in our favor.

There is an exodus that God is bringing to His people, but many people's souls have become so hurt and beat down that they have lost sight and vision and can't perceive that they are on the verge of a breakthrough. God has to take us the long way for a reason. Draw the strength, strategy, wisdom, and understanding you need from the Lord while you make intentional time in His presence. It's time to go from waiting to receiving.

"Then God said, "Behold, I am going to make a covenant. Before all your people I will perform miracles which have not been produced in all the earth nor among any of the nations; and all the people among whom you live will see the working of the Lord, for it is a fearful thing that I am going to perform with you." (Exodus 34:10)

241

Day 183

Secret Place

Don't give up in the middle of the process, even when some steps are harder to take than others. For we walk by faith and not by sight. Our feet become strong when we are founded and grounded in our secret place with God. God enlarges our steps as we continue to go up in His Presence. Even when we experience periods of being in the valley, God goes before us and after us as He covers our back. He places His hand of blessings on our head, as His Presence reassures us.

"Whoever dwells in the shelter of the Most High will rest in the shadow of the Almighty. I will say of the LORD, "He is my refuge and my fortress, my God, in whom I trust." *(Psalm 91:1-2)*

Call and trust that when you seek God throughout your process that you are heard, and He will come through for you. He says call on me, and I will answer. I will be with you in trouble. I will deliver you and honor you.

Scripture references: 2 Corinthians 5:7; Psalms 18:36; Psalm 139:5; Psalm 91:15

Day 184

Keys to My Heart

When we give God our hearts, He teaches us how to walk out our life with patience. We need patience towards ourselves and patience as we develop in our process. We have to allow God to mature us and use our minds wisely while we are coming out of whatever our valley is. Don't give up on making room for God because of your disappointments and feelings of discouragement.

Jesus is so serious about our lives, hearts, and emotions, or whatever else it is that we stand in need of, that He gave up his divine privileges; He took the humble position of a slave and was born as a human being. When He appeared in human form, He humbled himself in obedience to God and died a criminal's death on a cross. No matter how low you get or feel, remember that you still belong to God. You matter, and He calls you His very own. God's unexplainable love is what pulls us out of muck and miry clay. God's unexplainable love establishes our path and secures the way for us.

Scripture references: Philippians 2:7-8; 1 Corinthians 3:23; Psalm 40:2; Psalm 40:2

Prayer: Heavenly Father, let my heart be one that is guarded by peace, set on Heaven, and consistent and motivated to do the work that You have assigned me to do. Thank You in advance for bringing me out of every troublesome situation. I'm so grateful that I have a Savior who lives on the inside of me. Jesus, You are the treasure of my heart. You are ever present. No matter where I go, You are there. Your presence is powerful, and Your love is undeniable. In Jesus name I pray, Amen. (Philippians 4:7; Colossians 3:1; Colossians 3:23)

Day 185

Look No Further

Walk in your form of worship and keep it moving. Don't stop your God given tasks because of the tension you have been feeling in between the transition of your process.

"But this happened so that the works of God might be displayed in him." (John 9:3)

When things don't work out the way we think they should don't complain, give thanks. This is a heavy season of prevention and protection for those who have been diligent and faithful to God. As we go higher in our faith walk this is a sensitive time to not question the steps God has given you to take. Step out of your comfort zone and take the leap of faith. When you seek God you get a clearer view than what we can only see with our flesh and can comprehend with our mind.

I feel the Lord moving in my heart to tell His people, "Stop searching for what I have already given and provided to you." There is a time to search and a time to quit searching. A time to keep and a time to throw away." Peace is an inheritance that you don't have to wait to receive. Jesus said, Peace I leave with you; My peace I give you; I do not give to you as the world gives. Do not let your hearts be troubled and do not be afraid." When things go "wrong trust God enough that there's a blessing on the other side of it. God wants to bless His people in the overflow and keep us from being distracted from unnecessary stress and over worrying. Speak over yourself and say, "It's already getting better in the name of Jesus."

Scripture references: Ecclesiastes 3:6; John 14:27

Day 186

Grace Upon Grace

IT'S TIME TO ENTER IN! Enter into a new place. Enter into a new mind and way of thinking. Enter into leaving the past in the past. Enter into a place of forgiveness towards yourself and others. Enter into your season of healing and restoration. Enter into a place of rest. Enter into the assurity of who God says you are.

"Enter into His gates with thanksgiving, and into His courts with praise: be thankful unto Him, and bless His name (Psalm 100:2)".

It's a gift to be fully known and loved by God. So because God already knows us and is fully aware of our downfalls. For from His fullness we have all received, grace upon grace. We can't be afraid to put on righteousness, even when we think we're not good enough because Jesus already paid the price for our weaknesses and shortcomings. You don't have to keep trying to put on the rags of the past when God has called you to come out and walk in your NEW. It's because of Him that we can walk so close and intimate with God. The prayer for this devotion focus is that in everything we do let it lead us closer to the Cross, in Jesus name, Amen.

Scripture references: John 1:16; 1 Corinthians 6:20

Day 187
God's Approval

Pray about everything, including the "smallest" details of your life! The truth is we need God's blessing over everything concerning our lives. God's promises over our lives are Yes and Amen (2 Corinthians 1:20).

We can't truly succeed and last without God's approval, being that He supplies us life, health and strength to us. "Worship the Lord your God, and His blessing will be on your food and water. I will take away sickness from among you." (Exodus 23:25)

When God's blessing is on you, you can be confident that He hears you and is aware of the matters for your heart. "This is what the Lord, the God of your father David, says: I have heard your prayer and seen your tears; I will heal you." (2 Kings 20:5)

Day 188

Morning Has Come

You may have been in a season of weariness but it's time to come out! "My soul is weary with sorrow; strengthen me according to your word." (Psalm 119:28)

Your walk is getting ready to be different. You're getting ready to go from walking to leaping for joy! Not only is your walk getting ready to change but your voice is about to be filled with melodies from Heaven.

"He put a new song in my mouth, a song of praise to our God. Many will see and fear, and put their trust in the Lord". (Psalms 40:2)

God has compassion towards us.

"For His anger is but for a moment, His favor is for life; weeping may endure for a night, but joy comes in the morning." (Psalm 30:5)

Speak over yourself and say, "This is my season of joy, and my morning has come! Miracles are getting ready to take place all around me! In Jesus name, Amen."

Day 189

Faith and Obedience

Thank God for the unexplainable favor that's getting ready to hit your life. Only thing you're going to be able to say about what is getting ready to take place in your life when people ask is "God did it and you just have to experience Him yourself to even understand."

To experience the fullness of God, we have to surrender our will and agenda's and submit ourselves to God's Will and Agenda, allowing Him to totally have His Way. In order to let God have His way we have to move out of His way!

There is a consuming fire that has to hit our lives reaching the depths of our soul and the deepest form of our bellies where healing living waters flow (John 7:38).

In order for God to move how He wants to, the atmosphere has to be set. Our faith and obedience is what brings Glory to His name and causes blessings to come down.

Day 190
Victorious and Healed

We all have something big standing in front of us that we know only God can move and fix. Whatever that big thing is in your life that may be weighing on you, put it all on His shoulders today! When we think about something being placed on someone's shoulders, we can look at it as that person's responsibility to carry the weight of that specific thing. Placing your needs and cares on His shoulder guarantees your victory.

"But He was wounded for our transgressions; He was bruised for our iniquities. The chastisement of our peace was upon Him, and with His stripes we are healed." (Isaiah 53:5)

Day 191

Faith Fail Not

Don't let the exaggeration of the "truth" of your situation talk you out of believing that there is nothing left for you to be hopeful for. To be at a point where you feel there is no hope left means that all the faith you once had is not as strong as it once was. But there is someone who is praying for you so that your faith fail not. Jesus is always lifting you up before the Father.

"But I have prayed for you, Simon, that your faith may not fail. And when you have turned back, strengthen your brothers." (Luke 22:32)

When we think about being called to strengthen our brothers and sisters in Christ, we have to remember that there will be days when we have to encourage ourselves as well. The Word of God has to be the basis of the foundation in our encouragement.

Day 192
Fresh Oil

God is well concerned about us. He cares about His people and not only is He concerned but He loves with an unconditional and unfailing love. Because we know God is concerned about us, that is enough for us to learn to start praising instead of complaining. God's concern for us will cause us to be anointed with fresh oil because God does not leave His Children powerless.

"But my horn shall thou exalt like the horn of a unicorn: I shall be anointed with fresh oil." (Psalms 92:10 KJV)

Other Empowering scriptures for this encouraging word:

"For He will command His angels concerning you to guard you in ALL your ways; they will lift you up in their hands, so that you will not strike your foot against a stone." (Psalms 91:11-12)

"Teach us to number our days, that we may gain a heart of wisdom. Relent, Lord! How long will it be? Have compassion on your servants. Satisfy us in the morning with your unfailing love, that we may sing for joy and be glad all our days. Make us glad for as many days as you have afflicted us, for as many years as we have seen trouble. May your deeds be shown to your servants, your splendor to their children. May the favor of the Lord our God rest on us; establish the work of our hands for us, yes, establish the work of our hands." (Psalms 90:12-17)

Day 193

Bountiful Blessings

Don't empty yourself out because you are wasting energy on things you can't control. When you learn to build yourself up in God's word, you also learn to be careful with who or what you allow to tear you down. Don't waste what God has placed in you because others may not value or know how to handle and appreciate what's in you. God is watching over His word to be performed in your life.

Don't be distracted, keep yourself aligned with the Lord, so that you can stay in His will. Don't miss the performance of God because you're focusing on the distractions of the destroyer. Just like the devil tries to monitor your life and look for ways to devour you, God is watching over you, looking to perform what He has spoken. "I will sing of the Lord because He has dealt bountifully with me." Sing your song of deliverance and rest in the assurity of seeing God's deliverance over your situation. You may be lying down one way, but by the grace of God, you will rise in the morning in victory.

Scripture references: Jeremiah 1:12; 1 Peter 5:8; Psalm 121:5; (Psalm 13:6)

Day 194

Come Back

Even on a "bad" day, when you belong to God, no matter where you find yourself, there is grace for the place that you are in. You may have experienced some complications, but your situation is not too complicated for God. May you learn to rest with peace, knowing and believing that all things are going to come together and work for your good! You may feel downtrodden, but you are not forgotten. Your spirit can be uplifted even on your worst days and nights because God still has the best in mind for your life!

"Remember these things, O Jacob. Take it seriously, Israel, that you're my servant. I made you, shaped you: You're my servant O Israel, I'll never forget you. I've wiped the slate of all your wrongdoings. There's nothing left of your sins. Come back to me, come back. I've redeemed you." (Isaiah 44:21-22 MSG)

Day 195
The Advocate

God tells the sun to rise every morning. The sunrise signifies a new day, a fresh start, and light after a dark night. Many of us have had dark days but there is hope for us knowing that the sun has to shine again in our lives. You can rise on today because God is not just able, He's more than able to see you through. I pray that you will rise after what seems to be a dark season, that you will have hope again in Jesus name. You can rise because you have the Spirit of Christ in you. God wants to rid that helpless orphan spirit and mentality from us.

"I will not leave you as orphans; I will come to you." (John 14:18)

When we think about an orphan, we can compare him or she to not having anyone to advocate or care for them.

"But the Advocate, the Holy Spirit, whom the Father will send in my name, will teach you all things and will remind you of everything I have said to you. But the Advocate, the Holy Spirit, whom the Father will send in my name, will teach you all things and will remind you of everything I have said to you." (John 14:26)

Life sometimes may not always feel fair but be encouraged knowing you have someone advocating for you. Elohim, The God of Justice Himself.

Day 196

No More Silence

God wants to hear your voice for you. It's so easy to pray and believe for others in their time of suffering. But when it comes to us it's like we are at a loss for words. We will allow ourselves to suffer on account of our own unbelief, that God doesn't hear us or won't answer at all. God hears even the faintest cry (Psalms 34:17).

Our thoughts can trap us in a place God never called us to settle. Discouragement can be a dangerous place because it sometimes feels like you're sitting on a bench watching everyone's life and all the good things are just passing you by. We sometimes bench ourselves when we don't believe we can keep going or when we feel like we have messed up things with God in moments of weakness.

The Lord keeps calling us to take His hand as He reaches out to pull us up. Discouragement, guilt, and shame can eat away at us while our souls are starving and famished. To be spiritually famished with no consumption of God's word is to be spiritually malnourished. There is still hope, even when you have reached your lowest place.

We serve a good God who loves us even when we don't know how to love ourselves. We serve a good God who cares for us even when we don't know how to care for ourselves. We serve a God who will love us into our healing. The Holy Spirit helps us to get better; you don't have to wait to reach out to God when you think you have it all together.

"The Spirit and the Bride say, "Come." And let the one who hears say, "Come." And let the one who is thirsty come; let the one who desires take the water of life without price." (Revelation 22:17)

Day 197
Turbulence of Life

When the turbulence of life comes, God's grace and mercy help you to continue to soar through. Even at the sight of challenges and trials, strive to keep your eyes on your living hope, which is Jesus Christ, our Lord. Endurance is not about knowing that every step you take will always be the right one; it's about moving forward even when you don't always get it right and when things don't go as planned. Let this current test of faith and trust be one to grow you stronger in your relationship with God and not the one that makes you weaker due to fear, impatience, and unbelief for no word from God will ever fail.

Then Jesus told His disciples a parable to show them that they should always pray and not give up. Just because you are going through what seems to be test after test, it doesn't mean that your increase is not coming. If you don't give up, you will see increase and better days, like never before! Your future will be better than your past in the name of Jesus. Your beginning may have been small, but by the power of God's Word, your latter days will be great.

This increase will take you from being famished to flourishing. Situations may not have worked out in the past, but that doesn't mean your present and future won't work out. Don't let the past be proof that life will always be discouraging, but let it be proof of God's goodness being shown in your life as your life shifts for the better. The days that you have been waiting for are about to be in front of you.

Scripture references: John 16:33; Luke 1:37; Luke 18:1; Haggai 2:9; Job 8:7

Day 198
Everybody's Got a Reason

Continue to push yourself for you, or whatever your why is. Sometimes it can be a fight to even get out of bed for some people and face the responsibilities of life, but we still push anyway because there is a why attached to the reason we do what we do. Those internal battles where you feel like you can't go on, or no matter how hard you try to be positive, it's like a spirit of depression always tries to settle on you.

Depression is a branch that stems from the root of many factors, such as chemical imbalances in the brain and body, uncontrollable hardships, overwhelming negative circumstances, extremely stressful situations, rejection, genes, and environmental influences. Everyone's brain chemistry is wired and set up differently, and for some people, the constant mental battles often exhaust the body physically.

As you continue to walk out the rest of this week and shift into the weekend, just meditate and remind yourself of your WHY. God hears the silent whispers of your heart, and His Word reassures us that He will not let our foot slip (Psalm 121:3).

Our why give us a reason to go on. It's someone somewhere who needs you. Just show up, be you, and trust God in the process. Our battles may not make sense now, but when God brings us through, we will be able to help someone else who will have to go through what God has blessed us to overcome. When you live for God, as Christians, the reason we go on, our why, is on Christ's behalf.

> *"So I am well pleased with weaknesses, with insults, with distresses, with persecutions, and with difficulties, for the sake of Christ; for when I am weak [in human strength], then I am strong [truly able, truly powerful, truly drawing from God's strength]." (2 Corinthians 12:10 AMP)*

Day 199

Fourth Man in the Fire

This season is a season of gathering and preparation. We can go a lot further when we learn to recognize the difference between a problem and an inconvenience. Perspective matters and is important when choosing between the two. Maybe you have found your life in a mess, or even your emotions in a mess, or your circumstances are just a mess. God can gather you and place you on your feet! This encouraging devotion is about trusting in God to bring you into a new place of receiving even after the mishaps of life.

We go through misunderstandings, people hurt us, we hurt people, moments when life isn't fair, times when we have no clue which way to go, we may get a diagnosis we weren't expecting, finances seem to be in a dry place, you may lose people you never expected, and the long list of mishaps about life can go on. Even through the worst of things, we can still be encouraged and restored.

Adversity teaches us we can't escape pain or challenges. It helps us see that tough times are a blessing because they come with life, but they don't have to define who we are; instead, they can strengthen us to be better people. Adversity also teaches us to choose our battles wisely. We can't always change what has to happen to us, but we can change how we respond and go on after the mishaps of life happen to us.

God can preserve your harvest even after it's been tested and placed in the Fiery Furnace! As you read this devotion, make it personal and think of God's promises you know the Lord said would come to pass in your life. Just when you think you are about to go under, there is someone carrying you and walking alongside you in the fire. Jesus is our Fourth Man.

"Look!" He answered, "I see four men loose, walking in the midst of the fire; and they are not hurt, and the form of the fourth is like the Son of God (Daniel 3:25 NKJV)".

God loves us so much that He will split rocks on our behalf before He allows us to go under! When I think about rock being split, I think about breaking through a hard place. A place you maybe couldn't access before because it was too strong for you to overcome. God can lessen the strength and power of your enemies. The enemy of sickness, the enemy of defeat, the enemy of financial struggle, the enemy against whatever is standing in the way of your place of breakthrough. Our position in Christ can't be taken from us by anyone because we are born of His Spirit and washed in His blood. So, no matter what life throws at you, hold on to God, who is well aware of what you need and all your heart desires.

Day 200

Order My Steps

This devotion is a reminder that you are currently in a learning experience for your next! Which will be greater and require more! Keep your cool, and don't lose your head. In order to go to higher places, you have to be willing to humble yourself and know when to hold your peace. There will be situations that seem harmless but are a test, and whatever you choose to do and how you respond, let it result in peace. Even if you're upset or offended, let peace be your end goal. There is a positive you can pull out of every trying circumstance.

"When you live in a way that pleases the Lord, He makes even your enemies at peace with you (Proverbs 16:7)".

God has brought many of us too far to turn back now. Our dependence on God is what leads us into overflow. Turn to God with your empty cup! If you've been feeling empty, it doesn't have to be a bad thing. We serve a God who turns all things together for our good. God won't leave you hanging whenever you need Him the most. Jabez came before God with his empty cup and prayed for the Lord to fill it however He saw fit. Jabez cried out to the God of Israel,

"Oh, that you would bless me and enlarge my territory! Let your hand be with me, and keep me from harm so that I will be free from pain." And God granted his request (1 Chronicles 4:10)".

No matter our position in life, we need God's protection and blessing over everything we do. My prayer for us as the Body of Christ is that we will never lose connection with the Head, which is Christ. I pray that God will continue to order our steps and that we will follow His orders.

Day 201
Fasten the Belt of Truth

This devotion is about bringing focus to our thoughts. How we think can slow down our progress, and depending on how we respond to situations, it can complicate our process. Being held captive to your own mind and the things that have negatively affected you throughout your life can cause weeds to grow deeper and deeper into your garden.

Our bodies are a gift from God, and we have to tend to our mind and body as a garden. When we allow what happens around us to come in and trouble us, then we start to carry a burden for circumstances that are out of our control and damage the garden on the inside of us from growing healthily. When we are burdened, it affects who we are emotionally, mentally, physically, and spiritually if we don't "stand firm therefore, by fastening the belt of truth around your waist, by putting on the breastplate of righteousness." (Ephesians 6:14)

We have to grow to be mature enough in our faith that we don't allow troubles and burdens to negatively impact how we view God.

"Do not let your heart be troubled (afraid, cowardly). Believe [confidently] in God and trust in Him, [have faith, hold on to it, rely on it, keep going and] believe also in Me (John 14:1 AMP)".

Prayer: Heavenly Father, Bless me with the gift of faith, keep me from wavering and being double minded. Renew my desires Lord and strengthen me to continue in your faith grounded and settled in the Hope of the Gospel. Help me not to overlook you Lord, in the midst of difficulties and trials.

Thank you for being God. Your word tells us "For I the Lord do not change; therefore you, O children of Jacob, are not consumed (Malachi 3:6)". Thank you for a strengthened mind and heart that will continuously praise you. Holy Spirit, help me to think and speak positively. Help me to live an authentic life that reflects Jesus as my Lord and Savior. God forgive me for weeds known and unknown that I have let control my life. As You uproot what You did not plant in me, strengthen me to walk in my God given identity in Christ. In Jesus name, Amen.

Day 202

His Wonderful Light

This devotion is to bring a word of encouragement and prayer. It's important to learn to stand firm in our belief to receive from God and not talk ourselves out of our miracle that is yet to happen. When we talk ourselves out of our miracle, we are denying what the Lord can do. It's so easy to be so stuck and focused on our human ability that we can mistake God's ability. It is the Holy Spirit who gives people faith to recognize that Jesus is Lord (1 Corinthians 12:3). Faith restores our confidence in God, believing that anything is possible. Faith unites us with Jesus.

"Therefore, since we have been justified through faith, we have peace with God through our Lord Jesus Christ." (Romans 5:1 NIV)

A bad day or bad experience doesn't have to negatively shape your life or be the final result of how the rest of your life will go. Faith helps you see the Son (Romans 1:4) through dark skies. Faith calls your God given identity from the spirit realm into the earth. Claim what you want to see by faith.

"By faith, I believe I am getting ready to see a new level of myself, I am believing to see a new birth within me."

The version of ourselves that has been hiding under hurt, fear, setbacks, anxiety, worry, ongoing depression, warfare, negative thinking patterns, and emotional instability days are long over. We are going up before we go under! Well known scripture that speaks to our identity in Christ,

"But you are a chosen people, a royal priesthood, a holy nation, God's special possession, that you may declare the praises of him who called you out of darkness into his

wonderful light (1 Peter 2:9)."

You may be in a place where you feel like you are on the edge, but by faith, you are on the edge of your breakthrough. Faith has no bounds because God has no limits.

Prayer: Heavenly Father, let me be a person whose circumstances shape me to be a person of faith and not a person of fear. Lord, I thank you that your word is alive and active in my life (Hebrews 4:12). Let the intents of my heart be pure and let my motives be pure. In Jesus name, Amen.

Day 203

The Lifter of My Head

One thing about God, even when you are going through you don't have to question or wonder who you belong to. You are always wanted and treasure by God. Even when you're going through a crisis you can still have a hallelujah anyway. Even in your crisis there is still room for a divine appointment with God. You will not faint because the Lord will sustain you. God has an attentive ear to hear His people from His Holy Mountain. Things may be breaking and falling apart around you but your miracle is still on the way.

"But thou, O Lord, art a shield for me; my glory, and the lifter up of mine head. I cried unto the Lord with my voice, and he heard me out of his holy hill. Selah. I laid me down and slept; I awaked; for the Lord sustained me." (Psalms 3:3-5 KJV)

Day 204
His Perfect Timing

God doesn't waste our wounds; He uses them for the better. Pick yourself up and try again. Try again with whatever you have "failed," but go in with a mindset if "I am strengthened through Christ Jesus." (Philippians 4:13) God believes in you, even when you struggle to sometimes believe in yourself. Life can sometimes break us down with things that are not in our own "perfect plan."

We have to be broken to be molded and shaped by God's word. When life hurts and our thoughts are running deep into an unhealthy place, we have to be mindful and examine where our calm and comfort really lie. When we go through trying situations, it's not a matter of God's ability to come through, but our faith to believe in His perfect timing.

Prayer: Heavenly Father, Thank You for mercy. Jesus, Your Strength makes me new. "Behold, I was shapen in iniquity; and in sin did my mother conceive me. Behold, thou desirest truth in the inward parts: and in the hidden part thou shalt make me to know wisdom. Purge me with hyssop, and I shall be clean: wash me, and I shall be whiter than snow (Psalm 51:5-7 KJV)". In Jesus name, Amen.

Day 205

Take Comfort

This devotion helps us seek God for clarity. Don't give up on God because of what you may not understand right now. If you are in a place where you're like, "God, my heart hurts because so many things are unclear." Take comfort in knowing we serve a God whose light shines and brings truth into our lives. We all know what it's like to feel lost. So I want to encourage those who feel like they are in that lost place currently. When you are in a "lost" place, things can feel dark and lonely. Speak and pray this scripture when you feel like you are so consumed with worry; it will give you peace and break down the power of depression when it tries to settle on you.

"For the Son of Man has come to seek and to save that which was lost." (Luke 19:10)

God is reaching out to His people and giving them direction. He won't allow us to stay broken-hearted for too long.

Prayer: Heavenly Father, break the stronghold of unbelief off Your people's life. I pray for everyone who is in a dark place for God's divine radiance to light up what has been covered and hidden. Bring truth to our lives, Lord, for situations that's unclear, so that we can know how to pray and what to pray for. Reveal to us, God, what is necessary so that we can no longer fall victim to the enemy's tactics. The enemy of worry and anxiousness.

Oh, Lord, tear down every wall in our lives, shine light through every dark shadow. "God of Hope, fill us with Your joy and peace and increase our trust in You, so that we can overflow with hope by the power of the Holy Spirit. (Romans 15:13)

Thank You for Your unfailing love. God, I pray for my brothers and sisters in Christ right now who are drowning in grief and depression. Let them feel Your presence so strong in this hour, warm up their hearts, and let Your flow of love reach down to the deepest part of their being. Though the mountains be shaken, and the hills be removed, yet my unfailing love for you will not be shaken nor my covenant of peace be removed," says the LORD, who has compassion on you (Isaiah 54:10)". In Jesus name, Amen.

Day 206
Eye In The Sky

"For the eyes of the Lord are over the righteous, and his ears are open unto their prayers: but the face of the Lord is against them that do evil." (1 Peter 3:12)

Oh, how this Scripture ministers to me—His awareness over our lives. No matter the season we find ourselves in, whether it's day or night, His promises over our life will stand. I thank Jesus for His Heavenly Eye that's watching over His children. No matter where we find ourselves, we can't escape the Lord.

Many times in the Old Testament, God would come down in a dark cloud and speak. Clouds represent God's glory and appearance. I believe that many people's prayers are getting ready to be answered in the most divine and favorable ways. If this message ministers to you, have faith to believe that your time is now. I am expecting a mighty revival in this season of my life and yours too. I just want to see God's kingdom advance here on Earth. I want God to continue to make His children better people so that we can be a blessing to one another and not a curse.

I thank God for the colors of His glory. I am believing in God to make my life and the lives of my brothers and sisters in Christ more spiritually colorful so that we will be people found in good standing with the Lord.

"As it is written: The Spirit of the Lord will rest on Him, the spirit of wisdom and understanding, The spirit of counsel and strength, The spirit of knowledge and the fear of the Lord. And He will delight in the fear of the Lord, And

He will not judge by what His eyes see, nor make a decision by what His ears hear." (Isa. 11:2-3 NASB)

I believe it is a time of healing and restoration like never before. God is lifting many of His people up. There is a replenishing that is coming as we make ourselves available for God to fill us up. My prayer is that there will be special grace from the Lord that will cause us to walk differently, talk differently, and think differently. The grace that helps us as God's people to be more loving, compassionate, sincere, genuine, and authentic. The grace that helps us to serve better. The grace that helps us to be more spirit-minded. The grace that encourages us to endure and keep pressing. The grace that gives us the ability to sow cheerfully into one another lives as the Holy Spirit leads. In Jesus name, Amen.

Day 207

The Preeminence of Christ

God fashioned the Earth and holds it together. The same God created every person on this Earth and holds each of us together.

"Then the Lord God formed the man of dust from the ground and breathed into his nostrils the breath of life, and the man became a living creature." (Genesis 2:7)

He is the One who provides life, health, and strength. God knows what He is doing with our lives because He already has it planned out, along with the plans on how to take care of us. Wherever you find yourself in this moment, as you read this, be encouraged, knowing God is conscious of you. When we pray, we have to remember that God already knows about our problems, and He already has the solution for them. He's not up there in heaven worrying, trying to think of a plan on how to handle the situations that go on in our lives. Jesus' thoughts about His people are healing and life-changing.

"For I know the plans I have for you," declares the LORD, "plans to prosper you and not to harm you, plans to give you hope and a future." (Jeremiah 29:11)

He may not agree with our shortcomings and the works of the flesh that we fall into sometimes, but He provides us with a love that never runs out, which should make us want to do better as people and want God's glory to rise and settle among us. We need God's glory to rise among us because His presence will cause promotion in our lives. His glory will cause any hardened and cold heart to surrender.

His glory will cause your greatest enemies to bow down before you. His glory will cause a spirit of success to hit every area of your life that you have repeatedly failed in. His glory will cause people you don't know to feel led to bless you, His glory will cause people who once owed you, ducked, and dodged you to pay you back in full with interest, and His glory will cause double to hit your life after the enemy has stolen from you.

Scripture references: Isaiah 45:18, Colossians 1:17. Acts 17:25

Day 208
Longing for Eternity

The outcome you are worrying over is already in Jesus' hands.

Prayer Point: Holy Spirit, we need you to teach us how to pray and release and not pray and pick worry back up. If you have found yourself constantly running on E, you have to set a place within yourself to allow God to come and fill you.

The empty feeling we, as humans, have or will experience is a longing for something greater than what we are seeing here physically. We need the love of God, the peace of God to come into the gray areas of our lives and bring color into our souls. We can't allow our desperation for a specific outcome to cause us to create a counterfeit solution or outcome because we don't want to wait for God for the real thing.

Here are some examples from Scripture:

Sarah "created" her own outcome when she allowed Hagar to sleep with Abraham.

"So she said to Abram, "The LORD has kept me from having children. Go, sleep with my maidservant; perhaps I can build a family through her." Abram agreed to what Sarai said. So after Abram had been living in Canaan ten years, Sarai his wife took her Egyptian maidservant Hagar and gave her to her husband to be his wife." (Genesis 16:1-2)

To give the people of Israel water, Moses struck the rock with his staff instead of speaking to it like God commanded him to.

"Take the staff, and you and your brother Aaron gather the assembly together. Speak to that rock before their eyes

and it will pour out its water. You will bring water out of the rock for the community so they and their livestock can drink. So Moses took the staff from the Lord's presence, just as he commanded him. He and Aaron gathered the assembly together in front of the rock and Moses said to them, "Listen, you rebels, must we bring you water out of this rock?" Then Moses raised his arm and struck the rock twice with his staff. Water gushed out, and the community and their livestock drank." (Numbers 20:8-11)

We can't let the need for an outcome break our faith in God and cause us to be disobedient, removing ourselves out of God's will. Even when God has to rebuke us, we still have to continue to be faithful, honor God, and finish the work He has called to our hands. Trust in God to bring you to an expected end, giving you what you hoped for. Don't stop working on the things of God just because you have to wait a little while longer. Even in our waiting, God is able to give us what we truly need.

Day 209

Progression

Our encouragement in this devotion is pertaining to the Love of God. God's love will cause you to have peace with everyone, even when you want to raise sand. God's love teaches you wisdom on how to pick and choose battles, what conversations you should be willing to have, what conversations you're not willing to have in order to keep your own sanity, and how to avoid allowing situations to turn into something chaotic. God's love will cause you to think before you respond and not just react without thinking first. God's love produces a steadfast spirit in us.

Steadfastness causes you to stay in a path of progression, working towards the things of God. Stubbornness delays your progression because it doesn't open you up to God's way but only to what you currently see and feel based off of a hurt and bitter perspective. When we are steadfast we can look at tension as a way to promote us. When we are stubborn, tension adds fuel to a fire within us that's already deadly, awaiting an explosion.

> *"For this very reason, make every effort to add to your faith goodness; to goodness, knowledge, and to knowledge, self-control; and to self-control perseverance; and to perseverance, godliness and to godliness, mutual affection, and to mutual affection, love." (2 Peter 1:5-7)*

God's love teaches us that no matter how we're feeling there is always a reason to thank Him. God's love can find you in pain and brokenness but have the capability to nurse you back to joy and wholeness.

Prayer: Heavenly Father, Thank You for first loving me before I even knew You. God mold me into a vessel filled with your love. Teach me how to interact with others that have hurt me or will hurt me. Teach others how to interact with me if I have hurt them or will hurt them. Remove the spirit of envy and strife that may be trying to creep in and operate in my life. Bless my mind to be unwavering that no matter what I am facing I will serve you with gladness and not regret. Teach me how to humble myself in the Sight of You oh Lord. God, I bind up every spirit in Jesus' name sent to take my mind and destroy my destiny. God, I loose down a spirit of success from Heaven, success in every area of my life, in the name of Jesus. God, keep my soul from being closest to hell. In Jesus name, Amen.

Day 210

My Portion

Our word of encouragement is focused on increase. The first part of this message I want to challenge you to give to someone today. Sow into someone else's life using wisdom, as God leads you of course. Apostle C.C. Dixon often says, "God can't bless you with your hands close, you have to learn how to give."

"Give, and it will be given to you. Good measure, pressed down, shaken together, running over, will be put into your lap. For with the measure you use it will be measured back to you (Luke 6:38)."

Give a hug today, compliment someone, do something outside of your normal routine. The second part of this message is your increase comes from God not man.

"For promotion comes neither from the east nor the west nor from the south. But God is the judge: He takes one down from their position and raises another up." (Psalms 75:6-7)

I know others around you may be more well off than you as far as connections, resources and finances. People may have the upper hand because of certain positions that God has allowed them to be in but know that can change at any moment being that we can be up one day and down the next. God has the last say, He is the Author and Finisher of our faith (Hebrews 12:2). When God adds to your life there is no sorrow attached to it (Proverbs 10:22). When God moves in your life it produces a deeper level of praise and thankfulness. The more people look over you and push you to the side, the more God will increase you. "O Lord, I have so many enemies; so many are against me; you are my glory, the one who holds my head high.... Victory comes from you, O Lord (Psalms 3:1,3,8)".

Stay diligent in me says the Lord, and believe, I will do all that I have promised you. Look for an increase of peace, rest, new opportunities and doors. An increase of downloads in your mind to create. If you know this word is for you, pray and ask God what way he is increasing you and how you can best prepare for how He chooses to increase you. Be open and think big because an increase could mean the opposite of what you're thinking. Appreciate what form your increase will come in because that area God is multiplying you in is the key that's going to majorly shift your life and shoot you in a new direction. For His Glory claim it, increase is my portion in the name of Jesus!

ᗞay 211

Armor of Light

Draw near to God while the time is now for tomorrow is not promised to any of us.

"And that, knowing the time, that now it is high time to awake out of sleep: for now is our salvation nearer than when we believed. The night is far spent, the day is at hand: let us therefore cast off the works of darkness, and let us put on the armor of light." (Romans 13:11-12)

Now is not the time to be unstable and easily moved. Draw near to God who will give you fruits that will last. The enemy wants to keep us from producing Godly fruit. The enemy wants to tire people out so that we will draw back in fear, anger and bitterness keeping you from choosing God daily.

"You did not choose Me but I chose you, and appointed you that you would go and bear fruit, and that your fruit would remain, so that whatever you ask of the Father in My name He may give to you". (John 15:16)

It's dangerous when you are in a place of knowing who God is and have no excitement or reverence for him. There is a call for all people to draw near in your heart, it's more than just showing up physically. If our hearts are not where God is then the work that we do in the physical world holds no weight. When I meet God I don't want him to refuse me or anyone else striving towards the path of life when we think we have it right and we don't.

"Every tree that does not bear good fruit is cut down and thrown into the fire. Therefore you will recognize them by their fruits. Not everyone who says to me, 'Lord, Lord,' will enter the kingdom of heaven, but the one who does the

will of my Father who is in heaven. On that day many will say to me, 'Lord, Lord, did we not prophesy in your name, and cast out demons in your name, and do many mighty works in your name?' And then will I declare to them, 'I never knew you; depart from me, you workers of iniquity.' We build our house on the rock by hearing God's word and doing what we have learned. Everyone who hears these words of mine and does them will be like a wise man who built his house on the rock." (Matthew 7:19-24)

Day 212

Now Unto Him

Our devotion focus word for today is keep. The encouragement for the message is on keeping your inner peace flowing so you can keep yourself in alignment with God's will. God will keep in perfect peace those whose minds are steadfast, because they trust in Him. I keep my eyes always on the Lord. With him at my right hand, I will not be shaken. Make every effort to keep the unity of the Spirit through the bond of peace. The Lord will keep you from all harm, he will watch over your life; the Lord will watch over your coming and going both now and forevermore.

My child do not forget my teaching, but keep my commands in your heart, for they will prolong your life many years and bring you peace and prosperity (Proverbs 3:1-2).

It is the Lord your God you must follow, and Him you must revere. Keep His commands and obey Him; serve Him and hold fast to Him. The Lord bless you and keep you; the Lord make his face shine on you and be gracious to you; the Lord turn his face toward you and give you peace. But you, dear friends, by building yourselves up in your most holy faith and praying in the Holy Spirit, keep yourselves in God's love as you wait for the mercy of our Lord Jesus Christ to bring you to eternal life. Never be lacking in zeal, but keep your spiritual fire, serving the Lord. Now unto him that is able to keep you from falling, and to present you faultless before the presence of his glory with exceeding joy, to the only wise God our Savior, be glory and majesty, dominion and power, both now and ever. Amen.

Scripture references: Isaiah 26:3, Psalms 16:18, Ephesians 4:3, Psalms 121:7-8, Deuteronomy 13:4, Numbers 6:24-26, Jude 1:20-21, Romans 12:11, Jude 1:24-25

Day 213
God Who Justifies

This is a season where God is encouraging and nudging His children to face every fear. The supernatural strength you need will come from the Power of God. God is calling us out to do those things that we fear the most.

"For God has not given us a spirit of fear, but of power and of love and of a sound mind." (2 Timothy 1:7)

What move or gift has God instructed you to start in but you still remain seated on what you have been called to walk in?

"Do not be afraid of them or their hostile faces, For I am with you always to protect you and deliver you", says the LORD." (Jeremiah 1:8)

God is easing your anxious mind starting today! The Lord has granted you access and success! As you get in God's presence and continue to seek Him expect to see a change!

"My grace is all you need. My power works best in weakness (2 Corinthians 12:9)."

What was once standing in your way will fall.

"What then are we to say about these things? If God is for us, who is against us? He who did not withhold his own Son, but gave him up for all of us, will he not with him also give us everything else? Who will bring any charge against God's elect? It is God who justifies." (Romans 8:31-33)

Day 214

Worrying Adds Nothing

This encouraging message is on God's care. When you're thankful you realize you have more. Being unthankful takes away from the spirit of gratitude and it makes you feel like you have less and never satisfied, always in need of something. If you're always looking at what you don't have and who you don't have in your corner, it can make you feel like you never have enough.

You may not be where we want to be in life, but it's time that we all start being grateful for where we are. There is a quote that says, "I felt sorry for myself because I had no shoes, until I met a man who had no feet." Smile, show love and kindness to those you interact with daily, and be glad anyway. This is not to disregard how we feel because I know life can get hard, but being negative isn't going to help our case either when we are going through the trials of life. All things will work together in its timing.

"Does worry add anything to your life? Can it add one more year, or even one day? So if worrying adds nothing, but actually subtracts from your life, why would you worry about God's care of you?" (Luke 12:25-26 TPT)

Day 215
Armloads of Blessings

This season may have been challenging, warfare has increased intensely, hits after left and right but I am believing that we will see the manifestation of God's word prevail in our situations (Romans 1:16). We can hold on to the promise that God will take care of us! With the constant tests of faith, where you are currently planted God can still produce the blessing you need. It's easy to get discouraged and think what good can come out of this! But what I love about God is that He will allow His people to come out with more than what was lost.

This may have been a season of weeping, burdened by life, causing many tears. The hits many people have faced has caused a spirit of fear of failure and loss. You may have been down and out, but God is going to allow you out of those low feelings with a renewed fresh perspective. You are going to return with joy! Return to what? Your walk of faith. There is so much sorrow everywhere and we are constantly being presented with situations that can leave us troubled, but God will hold His people up so that our tears will be turned into unspeakable joy.

I believe that we have to go through discouraging situations so that we can learn how to properly handle discouragement. We have to learn to handle our troubles with God's word. God's word keeps our faith growing and our belief to be open for God to move in our lives with armloads of blessings!

"Those who sow in tears, shall reap in joy. He who continually goes forth weeping, bearing seed for sowing, shall doubtless come again with rejoicing, Bringing his sheaves with him." (Psalms 126:6)

Day 216

Connection to Christ

This devotion is an encouraging reminder that you are someone's connection to Christ! When you open up your heart to follow Jesus, you also get called into the mission of fishing for people.

"Come follow me,.... and I will make you fishers of men" *(Matthew 4:19).*

Your personality and life experiences make you perfect for the assignment God has given you. Even when we are frustrated, we have to commit to surrendering to Him and His desires for us. How many times have we found ourselves angry because of the obstacles we see in our path? And our focus becomes on all of our problems, not God. What happens to us when we get what we thought we wanted, and it wasn't what we expected? We become frustrated and complain. If you find yourself here, pray for realignment to what His plans are for your life in this current season.

"Sow righteousness for yourselves, reap the fruit of unfailing love, and break up your unplowed ground; for it is time to seek the Lord, until he comes and showers His righteousness on you" *(Hosea 10:12).*

Go forward, not allowing fear to keep you from reaching the new horizon God desires for you. How far would God go to reach our hearts? He was willing to send His very own Son (John 3:16) that we can become His very own sons and daughters through the adoption of Jesus Christ (Ephesians 1:5).

Call out to God and ask Him to bless you in every way you

need. After a season of extended and painful wrestling with God (Genesis 32:22-23), we gain a fire in us that is stirred by the endurance to persevere in prayer and seeking God's face.

Our tests in life help us to reflect upon ourselves, whether we will hold on to God or give up. By faith we hold on to God and don't let go until He blesses our soul (Genesis 32:26).

Day 217

Hope Prevails

This devotion allows us to focus on the fact that God is a Man of His Word. God expects us to believe when He speaks concerning our lives.

"If we are faithless [do not believe and are untrue to Him], He remains true (faithful to His Word and His righteous character), for He cannot deny Himself". (2 Timothy 2:13 AMP)

"Blessed be the Lord, Who has given rest to His people Israel, according to all that He promised. Not one word has failed of all His good promises which He promised through Moses His servant." (1 Kings 8:56 AMP)

There is a rest God has for us to enter according to His promises. Why is it so hard to take hold of God's rest? Is it because we struggle to believe what God has said will come to pass because we are currently going through the opposite of what was spoken?

"So shall they fear the name of the Lord from the west, and his glory from the rising of the sun. When the enemy shall come in like a flood, the Spirit of the Lord shall lift up a standard against him." (Isaiah 59:19)

Just because you are currently going through challenges, it doesn't mean God is not mindful of His covenant with you and that you are not in His heart.

"He is [earnestly] mindful of His covenant and forever it is imprinted on His heart, the word which He commanded and established to a thousand generations." (Psalms 105:8 AMP)

Another aspect of entering into God's rest and peace is believing who He says we are. If you feel unlovable, God says you are forever loved. You are not too difficult, damaged, or messed up that no one could ever love you and be patient with you. We may feel weak, but God makes us strong. We recognize that we are sinners, but God says we are forgiven. We may feel abandoned by people, but God says we have been adopted. We may feel broken, but God says He makes us whole. We may have experienced rejection, but God says we are His.

We may feel alone at some points in our journey, but God says He is with us. We sometimes feel hopeless, but God says we are hopeful through Him. We say we feel lost at times, but God says He gives us direction. We go through experiences that make us unhappy, but God says we are joy filled. We sometimes feel afraid, but God says we have power, we are loved, and have a sound mind. If you feel unwanted or like nothing special, God says you are fearfully and wonderfully made.

Scripture references: Romans 8:38-39, Psalms 18:32, 1 John 2:12, Ephesians 1:5, Colossians 2:10, Isaiah 43:1, Joshua 1:9, Jeremiah 29:11, Isaiah 30:21, John 15:11, 2 Timothy 1:7, Psalms 139:14)

Day 218
Faith in Times of Distress

We have an empowering word reminding us to look to the Lord for strength. In our heartaches God is with us. God is patient with us in every step we take along the way. His patience for us comes from Him not wanting anyone to perish but for everyone to come to repentance (2 Peter 3:9). Jesus comforts His people even when He has to correct us. God does everything in love with each of us in mind (Psalms 8:4).

"Let not your heart be troubled; you believe in God, believe also in Me. In My Father's house are many mansions; if it were not so, I would have told you. I go to prepare a place for you. And if I go and prepare a place for you, I will come again and receive you to Myself; that where I am, there you may be also. And where I go you know, and the way you know." (John 4:1-4)

There is a battle within to do what's right.

"So I find this law at work: Although I want to do good, evil is right there with me. For in my inner being I delight in God's law; but I see another law at work in me, waging war against the law of my mind and making me a prisoner of the law of sin at work within me. What a wretched man I am! Who will rescue me from this body that is subject to death? Thanks be to God, who delivers me through Jesus Christ our Lord! So then, I myself in my mind am a slave to God's law, but in my sinful nature a slave to the law of sin." (Romans 7:21-25)

This devotion is to encourage each of us just because we are in a battle not to give up on ourselves. God's word encourages us to keep in step with the Spirit. (Galatians 5:16-18)

Prayer: Hear me when I call, O God of my righteousness! You have relieved me in my distress; Have mercy on me, and hear my prayer. "Give ear to my words, O Lord, Consider my meditation. Give heed to the voice of my cry, My King and my God, For to You I will pray." (Psalms 4:1; Psalm 5:1-3)

"O Lord do not rebuke me in Your anger, Nor chasten me in Your hot displeasure. Have mercy on me, O Lord, for I am weak; O Lord, heal me, for my bones are troubled. My soul also is greatly troubled; But You, O Lord—how long? Return, O Lord, deliver me! Oh, save me for Your mercies' sake (Psalms 6:1-4)!" In Jesus name, Amen.

Day 219

Ruach Elohim

This fresh, encouraging word is full of wisdom. We need God to hover over us. When He hovers over us, we receive life, strength, order, and beauty from what is a mess in our lives, even the aspects of ourselves we think is good. We need God's presence to hold us up and cleanse us daily. When God hovers over us He turns what's chaotic into a promise.

If you are feeling empty, ask God to hover over you. If you need strength, ask God to hover over you. If you need healing, ask God to hover over you. If you need peace, ask God to hover over you. If you are feeling lonely, ask God to hover over you. If your life is chaotic, ask God to hover over you. If you are struggling with addiction, ask God to hover over you. If you are struggling with lust and fornication, ask God to hover over you.

If you struggle with overeating, ask God to hover over you. If you struggle with overthinking, ask God to hover over you. If you lack self-control and discipline, ask God to hover over you. If you are sinking in the pit of depression, ask God to hover over you. If you are in need of comfort, ask God to hover over you. Whatever you need, just ask God to hover over you.

Here is a few scriptures on Hover for this devotion:

Isaiah 11:2 MSG, "The life-giving Spirit of God will HOVER over him, the Spirit that brings wisdom and understanding, The Spirit that gives direction and builds strength, the Spirit that instills knowledge and Fear-of-God ".

Genesis 1:2, "And the earth was a formless and desolate emptiness, and darkness was over the surface of the deep, and the Spirit (Ruach) of God was HOVERING over the surface of the waters".

Isaiah 31:4-5, "This is what GOD told me: "Like a lion, king of the beasts, that gnaws and chews and worries its prey, Not fazed in the least by a bunch of shepherds who arrive to chase it off, So GOD-of-the-Angel-Armies comes down to fight on Mount Zion, to make war from its heights. And like a huge eagle hovering in the sky, GOD-of-the-Angel-Armies protects Jerusalem. I'll protect and rescue it. Yes, I'll HOVER and deliver."

Day 220

Stirred to Soar

The focus scripture for the highlight of this word is coming from Deuteronomy 32:11-12, "Like an eagle that stirs up its nest and hovers over its young that spreads its wings to catch them into the air, teaching them to fly. The Lord alone led His people, and there was no foreign god helping them."

Our hard places allow God to develop us to be a people ready to conquer everything the Lord has promised us. An eagle teaches their young how to by pushing them out of the nest so that they can try to use what they were born with, which is their wings. Like us, there are qualities and gifts written over our lives from the beginning of time, and we have to learn how to use what's been given unto us.

Sometimes we don't know how to use what we were born with until it's the only choice we have left. The mother eagle doesn't leave the baby eaglets to look after themselves; even when she pushes them out into the deep, at the right moment and time, she knows when to swoop down and allow her children to drop onto her wings and carry them back into the nest.

In verse 11, we see this example in our everyday lives. God takes us from a place of captivity and downheartedness and shifts us into circumstances that are a little less worse than where we came from and temporarily leaves us there to teach us how to depend on Him in the unimaginable. God makes our troubles not so bad when we know that He is there with us through it.

God remains with us to give us strength, security, guidance, peace, and protection, even when He is teaching us how to fly. God knows when to provide the necessary change, when to make things uncomfortable to bring us to a point of maturity and come into adulthood. Just like the mother eagle, God knows that if He doesn't stir our nest by testing our faith and teaching us how to trust Him in our hard situations, we, just like the baby eagles, wouldn't have the desire to learn how to fly if we were not pushed out of our "safe zone."

Without a disruptive environment that takes us out of our norm, we will not grow, adapt, and develop the necessary abilities to survive and thrive. Though the stirring of our nest may be painful and uncomfortable, it is still a gift wrapped for us to gain life, faith, and the ability to soar. Isaiah 40:31 says, "But they that wait for the Lord shall renew their strength; they shall mount up with wings like eagles; they shall run and not be weary; they shall walk and not faint."

We have to be stirred to walk into the good works prepared beforehand (Ephesians 2:10). When times are tough and you are being persecuted do not throw away your confidence, your faith, and trust in God, for you will be richly rewarded (Hebrews 10:35). You need to persevere so that when you have done the will of God, you will receive what He has promised (Hebrews 10:36). We are God's righteous one who will live by faith. God takes no pleasure in those who shrink back (Hebrews 10:38).

But we do not belong to those who shrink back and are destroyed, but to those who have faith and are saved (Hebrews 10:39). God knows about every struggle we will have to endure. He understands our human weakness that the imprint of this world would bring.

"And you were dead in the trespasses and sins in which you once walked, following the course of this world, following the prince of the air, the spirit that is now at work in the sons of disobedience—among who we all once lived in the passion of our flesh, carrying out the desires of the body and the mind, and well by nature children of wrath,

like the rest of mankind. But God being rich in mercy, because of the great love which He loved us even when we were dead in our trespasses made us alive together with Christ, by grace you have been saved and raised up with Him and seated us with Him in the Heavenly places in Christ Jesus." Ephesians 2:1-6

God knew mankind needed a savior, someone who could show us the way of life and how to live a lifestyle pleasing to Him. So Jesus was sent for you and me. Hebrews 1:3, "Jesus is the radiance of the glory of God and the exact imprint of His nature, and He upholds the universe by the word of His power. After making purification for this, He sat down at the right hand of the Majesty on High." Jesus imparted to us the resemblance of our God given identity as children of the Most High God.

Day 221

The Song of Moses

The scripture passage for this devotional prayer is coming from Deuteronomy 32:1-6, 10,12,16-20.

Prayer: Heavenly Father, Your word calls us to attention. Listen you heavens and I will speak; hear, you earth the words of my mouth (v.1). Lord, let Your teaching fall like rain and Your words descend in our hearts and minds like dew, like showers on new grass, like abundant rain on tender plants (v.2). Lord, help us to proclaim Your name and praise the goodness of God (v.3). You are our Rock, God, Your works are perfect and all Your ways are just. You are a faithful God who does no wrong, upright and just, You are Lord (v.4).

Help us not to be a part of a corrupt and fatherless generation in the Spirit. Don't allow us to be put to shame, keep us from being bent or twisted out of shape and a crooked generation. Save the souls closest to hell (v.5). Help us not to repay Your goodness by being foolish and unwise. You are our Father and Creator, You made and formed us Oh, God. We don't want to take you for granted (v.6).

Lord, let us never forget where you found us. In a helpless condition, in a desert land, barren and howling waste. Desolate in the spiritual and physical. But You Lord, shield and care for us constantly, guarding us as the apple of your eye (v.10). You alone guide Your people, You are God all by Yourself. Keep us away from foreign gods and idols, nothing or no one compares to You and will be able to bring us through the trials of life successfully like You can God (v.12).

Help us not to be people who benefit off of Your Goodness, then forsake You. Help us not to stir You to jealousy with strange and foreign gods with abominations, let us not provoke you to anger (v.16). Keep us from being a people that sacrifices to demons, to gods we never knew, to new gods that had recently come (v.17). Help us to be people after Your heart. Help us to never desert You, You are always mindful of us and father us daily, You are the God who gave birth to us and supplies life (v.18).

Don't reject us, Oh God, nor turn Your face from us. Help us not to be sons and daughters that anger you (v.19). Keep us from being a perverse generation, children who are unfaithful (v. 20). Thank You God for Your Heart of Generosity. Sanctify our hearts, Lord. Sanctify our minds, Lord. Sanctify our lives, Lord. Thank You for Your Breath in our lungs. You are the God who restores every heart that is broken. There is only one name with power to save, we thank You for Your Great name Jesus. You reign forever more Lord. Be glorified in our hearts, Lord. Glorify Your name in our lives, Lord. In Jesus name, Amen.

Day 222

Spiritual Lamp

The focus for this message is on making the most of our time. Ephesians 5:15-17, "Be very careful, then, how you live—not as unwise but as wise, making the most of every opportunity, because the days are evil. Therefore, do not be foolish, but understand what the Lord's will is."

If we are not careful with how we spend our time daily, we could fall away in our relationship with God. How are we making sure daily that we keep oil in our spiritual lamp so that our light won't go out? If we let our light go out with Jesus, then we lose hope and spiritually decay. Our lives should yield to God's will and Lordship.

For if we live, we live to the Lord, and if we die, we die to the Lord. So then, whether we live or whether we die, we are the Lord's (Romans 14:8). If we are not yielding to God, then we are yielding to sin and our flesh, living a life not pleasing to Him, allowing bad habits to take over us and have their way in our lives.

Our spiritual oil only increases by seeking God for ourselves and devoting ourselves to God's will. Not everyone who says to Me, 'Lord, Lord,' shall enter the kingdom of heaven, but he who does the will of My Father in heaven. Many will say to Me in that day, 'Lord, Lord, have we not prophesied in Your name, cast out demons in Your name, and done many wonders in Your name?' And then I will declare to them, 'I never knew you; depart from Me, you who practice lawlessness." (Matthew 7:21-23)

Prayer: Heavenly Father, Thank You for being the Father of Heavenly Lights. I can walk through this dark world with The

Holy Spirit illuminating God's word to help me see. You are my lamp, Oh Lord; You turn my darkness into light (2 Samuel 22:29). The light of the righteous rejoices, but the lamp of the wicked will be put out (Proverbs 13:9).

You are a Holy God and I need you to burn every wicked desire out of me. Jesus, Your anointing oil is what gives my lamp light, let your Presence overflow in me. I know it's time where I mess up God because no one is perfect, only You Lord. Keep me off the path of destruction.

"For we all have become like one who is [ceremonially] unclean [like a leper], And all our deeds of righteousness are like filthy rags; We all wither and decay like a leaf, And our wickedness [our sin, our injustice, our wrongdoing], like the wind, takes us away [carrying us far from God's favor, toward destruction]". (Isaiah 64:6)

You are the God of Grace and Mercy. I acknowledge You as King in my life and I acknowledge myself as a new creation covered by the blood of Jesus. I pray for those who don't yet believe that God may grant them the gift of repentance leading to salvation. In Jesus name I pray, Amen.

Day 223

Teach Me to Number My Days

Our inspiration today comes from Psalms 90:12, "Teach us to number our days, that we may gain a heart of wisdom." This message also piggybacks off yesterday's encouragement on making the most of our time. We need wisdom to be taught how to use our time wisely for God. We number our days by living a life that counts. Our time here on earth is short and brief.

"My son, if you accept my words and store up my commands within you, turning your ear to wisdom and applying your heart to understanding, indeed, if you call out for insight and cry aloud for understanding, and if you look for it as for silver and search for it as for hidden treasure, then you will understand the fear of the Lord and find the knowledge of God. For the Lord gives wisdom; from his mouth comes knowledge and understanding. He holds success in store for the upright, he is a shield to those whose walk is blameless, for he guards the course of the just and protects the way of his faithful ones. Then you will understand what is right, just and fair, every good path (Proverbs 2:1-9)".

We need wisdom when it comes to our purpose, so that we won't become idle. Luke 12:19-21, "And I'll say to myself, "You have plenty of grain laid up for many years. Take life easy; eat, drink, and be merry."" "But God said to him, 'You fool! This very night, your life will be demanded from you. Then who will get what you have prepared for yourself?' "This is how it will be with whoever stores up things for themselves but is not rich toward God."

Prayer focus is coming from passage Psalms 90:1-17: Lord,

you have been our dwelling place in all generations. Before the mountains were brought forth, or ever you had formed the earth and the world, from everlasting to everlasting you are God. You return man to dust and say, "Return, O children of man!" For a thousand years in your sight are but as yesterday when it is past, or as a watch in the night. You sweep them away as with a flood; they are like a dream, like grass that is renewed in the morning; in the morning it flourishes and is renewed; in the evening it fades and withers. For we are brought to an end by your anger; by your wrath we are dismayed. You have set our iniquities before you, our secret sins in the light of your presence.

For all our days pass away under your wrath; we bring our years to an end like a sigh. The years of our life are seventy or even by reason of strength eighty; yet their span is but toil and trouble; they are soon gone, and we fly away. Who considers the power of your anger, and your wrath according to the fear of you? So teach us to number our days so that we may get a heart of wisdom.

Return, O Lord! How long? Have pity on your servants! Satisfy us in the morning with your steadfast love, that we may rejoice and be glad all our days. Make us glad for as many days as you have afflicted us, and for as many years as we have seen evil. Let your work be shown to your servants, and your glorious power to their children. Let the favor of the Lord our God be upon us, and establish the work of our hands upon us; yes, establish the work of our hands! In Jesus name I pray, Amen.

Day 224
Labor of Love

This inspirational devotion is focused on the labor of love. As the body of Christ, we have to go through to help others get through. The foundation of our labor should be Christ and not for our own glory. When all that we do is Christ centered and we do it wholeheartedly, we work up a spiritual sweat. We travail for those that are assigned to us, until Christ is fully developed in their lives (Galatians 4:9). We all need faithful travailing people in our lives to pray and cover us as Christ continues to form himself in us.

Each time we deny ourselves, pick up our cross and follow Jesus, push in prayer, worship instead of worry, praise instead of complaining, share our testimonies, become doers and not just hearers, each time we encourage and share the Word of God with someone, we gain more momentum in the Lord. Our steadiness and momentum in God are what allow us to go from faith to faith, strength to strength, and glory to glory.

"But, beloved, we are confident of better things concerning you, yes, things that accompany salvation, though we speak in this manner. For God is not unjust to forget your work and labor of love that you have shown toward His name, in that you have ministered to the saints and do minister. And we desire that each one of you show the same diligence to the full assurance of hope until the end, that you do not become sluggish, but imitate those who through faith and patience inherit the promises," (Hebrews 6:9-12).

Don't stop praying, don't stop believing, and most of all, don't stop trusting in God. He is able to bring each of us through; read Psalms 18 to help uplift you while you await God's deliverance. Our encouragement is a reminder that God is with us in the fire. He's with us when we are feeling those labor pains from spiritual births taking place. When spiritual births in Christ take place, God touches our spirit and confirms who we really are. He is our Father, and we are His children. We then can receive the Spirit of Adoption and are freed from the spirit of bondage, which keeps us in fear and constantly condemning ourselves.

Day 225
Call to Worship

No matter the trial, you will not be overtaken. The weapons may form against your mind, health, money, family, ministry, and anything connected to you, but it will not prosper in taking you out. When you have God within you, He won't let you fall to the point of no return. God sees you and your trials. Your trials are building you for what it is you are expecting to receive from the Lord.

You can still prosper if you are at an unfamiliar place in your life by your communication with God. Communication with God keeps you in alignment for the assignment. We have to learn to make worship a daily practice. Each of us is on different levels within our spiritual journey. It's so easy to become discouraged that it becomes our first response, and that response becomes a cycle that leads to a pit of emptiness and despair.

Our trials can become teachers of life, and we learn how to make worship to God our first response. Our first response to life should automatically be to go to God, being devoted in prayer with a heart of thanksgiving even when our circumstances are at their worst.

Scripture references: Isaiah 54:17; Psalms 46:5; Colossians 4:2

Day 226
Connected To The Source

Don't lose sight of who you are and whose you are just because you're going through a tough battle. Even in a desolate place, you are not a desolate person because you're still a part of God's remnant. God says, "I myself will gather the remnant of my flock out of all the countries where I have driven them and will bring them back to their pasture, where they will be fruitful and increase in number. Prayer keeps you connected to God.

Your name and identity in God don't change, neither does God change when things are not going so well. Because God is constant and ever-present, He allows us to not be consumed. God has given us the power in our voice to speak His word to every desolate place and call forth life.

Your desolated place may be depression, feelings of emptiness, health issues, financial problems, or attacks of the mind. Whatever it is, God still favors you, and you will come out victorious. As you reflect and look back over your life, you will see how God has been with you all along. He's reliable and faithful!

"Yet for us there is [only] one God, the Father, Who is the Source of all things...." You are connected to the Source, which means you are blessed in the city, blessed in the field, blessed when you come, and blessed when you go.

Scripture references: Jeremiah 23:8; Malachi 3:6; 1 Corinthians 8:6; Deuteronomy 28:3, Deuteronomy 28:6

Poetry

A Woman Empowered By Love

I am a woman,
a passionate woman driven by love.
A love so intimate that pours down
from up above.
I'm connected to Heaven,
by the Spirit of the Heavenly Dove.

If you ask me how I feel today,
I would tell you that I'm overflowing with joy
knowing that every day
I experience unconditional love.

Peace is my crown and treasure
lies in my smile.
The virtue of who I'm becoming,
Flows deeper than the depths of the ocean.

I am a Phenomenal Woman who
has experienced many hurts.
My hurts don't define my worth. What defines me
is who God spoke over me to be before my feet
ever touched the Earth.

Treasure In Jars of Clay

When I'm feeling gray Jesus
Adds color to my life
When I'm feeling cloudy Jesus
Is my light that shines like the sun

And my Star that guides me
Through the night
Let your word shoot from
Heaven like an arrow
Arresting and ruling over every
Darkness in the Earth

Thank you for being the anchor of my soul
From the beginning to the end
You always hold me up when I'm down
A love that sustains after a thousand
generations

One savior who died facing a criminal's
Penalty without hesitation
A love that upholds my heart when
I'm facing my darkest day
I looked up and there was Grace

Love and forgiveness awaits
Me to face another day
Jesus is the treasure to my heart
Even unto my last breath
I'm still In His Hands

In His Hands

Only God is able to hold me through the night
When fear surrounds me, remind me that
I'm precious in your sight
And that I'm covered in the
power of your might

Touch my plans with Your Divine Hands
Keep me out of the enemies camp and from
wandering in the wilderness
God, I thank You for being faithful
to the faithless

Your love reminds me to be of good cheer
God is with me, He is always near
My trouble won't consume me
because I'm In His Hands

There is a time when I have to lift my head
because I'm in His Hands
The gate of my heart has to open
because even it lies In His Hands
Every wound and heartbreak is In His Hands
The pain I can't always explain is
In His hands

Jesus you are my Lighthouse,
I can look up to You and safely
make it back to shore
Because I'm in Your Hands Lord,
You remind me that I've been
redeemed and restored

Incapable to God is Able

When my inadequacies speak to me
It doesn't change the fact that God
called and speaks over me
God's word turns my "I can't" into "I can"

Even when my heart goes on
with a silent rant about my "insignificance"
God himself qualifies me
He clothes me in Grace

He trades the ashes of who I was
For the beauty of who I'm becoming
My heart now beats for the purpose
God has placed in me

It's my hope when I feel alone
From walking with those feelings that lead
to a trail where broken hearts resides
My confidence remains in my Savior

Who strengthens me so I won't
remain in faith that wavers
I then grasp on to the peace that Jesus
left for me and gave freely for my trouble
as He rose in victory

My incapable transforms into capable
because God is able to do exceeding
abundantly above all
which makes me unbreakable

311

Tiaina Doughty

No Longer Bound, I am Free

The power of God is taking me up,
I am no longer bound
Though isolation feels so real,
I thought I would never be found

Found outside my mind or lost in time
Oh, How I prayed and plead the blood
of Jesus over my mind

In the lowest of my darkest place,
I called out to God
He pulled me out of the elements of darkness,
ensuring me that I am safe in His arms

From Glory to Glory I go
At each level as I go higher,
the Lord makes me more beautiful
Beautiful in His Grace, Strength and Might

Look at my life now such a pleasant sight
No more chains holding me
Freed from the chains of shame
Jesus, Oh how I love His name
No longer bound, I am Free

Light in the Darkness

We never have to be scared of the dark
Because wherever the light shines,
There you always are

Whether it's through tunnel vision or
airplane lanes your constant love lights up
our lives and we never remain the same

We step into something and never know
what to expect but what's in the dark is less
scary when we know the One who we are
walking with

We only fear the dark because
Of what we can't see but as we hold on to
your right hand you assure us it's the safest
place to be

In the dark season you show us
The greatest mysteries ever told
Heaven's secrets are in front of our eyes,

Awaiting for us to behold, like the stars
twinkling above in the 5am skies
Oh, how I appreciate your love and
Being the apple of your eye

Broken on the Ground

Lead me to the Rock
That Spoke Let there be light
And Peace on Earth
When the Lord wants to add someone to your life
Whether it's for some moments or a lifetime
All is takes is one second to confront the unexpected
That turns our hectic to a positive perspective

The Lord sent you to me
He sent what I needed
Words and a hug
That all began with a tug
God cares about what worries us
He cares about those emotions we carry around

When we're broken on the ground
Even when we think no one sees us
That pain that brings us to our knees
While tears form and our heart cries out loud,
Oh God help me please

Then the Holy Spirit comes in with a comfort
That compares to no other
Will we open up even when we are
used to being closed off
With our back is against the wall

Whenever we are faced with giants
and expecting the impossible
The Lord sends people to remind you

that everything is going to be alright.

Just as is Holy word projected
All things work together for our good
When we just let Him
Even when we don't understand
When we are in the midst of trouble

Jesus takes hold of our hand that
lifts us higher than any romance
No matter how trying the situation,
I am reminded that Jesus sacrificed
His life for me with no hesitation

What God starts in us He will complete
When others was careless with my life
Even when I was careless with my life
Jesus You were there and cared the whole time
All along I've been searching for peace
And Jesus said Peace be still all along

When I look back over my life I've always been yours
There's never been a time where You wasn't available
When we rise up in the Lord's strength
It shows that depression and
anxiety doesn't have ownership

Even though sometimes it's like I can't get past me
Thoughts of failure seems to be on repeat
My inner enemy constantly making mischief
I sometimes feel like hiding from myself
Because of the thoughts within me

Crucify My Pain

What do you do when it hurts so bad that
you don't want to face what's real
I would rather not feel what is it that I feel
I try to convince myself that my pain is not real
But the emptiness speaks louder than denying how I feel

Leaving out of God's presence,
I shouldn't feel the same
But better than when I first came
I have so much frustration and disappointment
built up on the inside of me that its left untamed

The truth is my heart screams for love
wishing to be saved from pain
Why can't I just grasp God's grace
The One who loves me unashamed
and breaks every chain

What Jesus offers is free and easy to obtain
In the midst of all my striving,
I forget that I'm not the one driving
My life is not my own, Jesus thought
I was worth dying for

Where I am now does not
measure to where I'm going
The truth is God knows every part of me
and understands me better than I understand me
I can rest in the fact that He loves me perfectly
That vulnerable part of me that's crying to be held

Truthful Eyes

Be you, love you, forgive you.
I know it hurts, but you can go on another day.
You're not alone, never alone, it's always another way.
Don't cheat yourself out of life, if you end it now, you will
never see the chance of things being made right.

I know it hurts, you question yourself.
"Can I trust myself or should I just be someone else?"
We've been in denial, who's gonna help
this innocent child. Trapped on the inside;
It's ok to have broken pieces in
a world built on perfection.

Your heart has been crying out for redirection.
You've been raging for a long time. I seen your rage
that's quiet and not as loud as the roaring lion.
But the rage that's stuck between your mind and time
Hidden behind glossy eyes, drunken lips, addictions, and
spreaded thighs.

The eyes, they never lie,
even if your lips spoke 1,000 times,
your eyes hold the truth behind every hidden lie.

Goodbye Little Me

Goodbye little me no more
holding me back from my destiny
The kid on the inside who's
faced rejection and toxic tendencies

Trauma and abandonment issues won't
drive my internal ship recklessly
God, I'm calling for you to take the
wheel and guide my vessel carefully

I will no longer allow fear to keep me
from praying to the heavenlies
God is awaiting to open house and
to reveal hidden treasuries

Heaven has my recipe
More than just open sesame
But the key to my flesh and sin to no
longer be the death of me

My pain doesn't have to take me
to a place that I reach my highest ecstasy
Whether it's drugs and substances
or getting my "healing" sexually

Ahhh, I got to get some therapy
I'm in need of divine clarity
No more of what the world
offers me temporarily

Hope That Never Fades

God's word is my weaponry
Hallelujah is my melody
I'm building a Godly harvest and
triumphant will be my legacy

My pain has a message that
will speak to my ministry
Goodbye little me the Holy Trinity
has changed my whole trajectory

The Little Things

Getting past the little things
When I "forget" who I am as if Christ
isn't embedded in me

I feel myself wading lost wandering
into the everglades,
a lost shallow part of my mind.
While my feet tread to hallow ground
swift as a red hind

Walking wavered over a bridge,
how could I forget the compartment of privilege
That I can hang up my past releasing
the rope of backwardness

I am a gift and reward by Christ's heritage
Matched again with the toughest decision
Pulling the trigger back on my emotions
as my thoughts come rushing fast as a bullet

Those feelings that erupt quick
like a loose cannon
My roots run deeper than the cedar of Lebanon
I'm above ground, In the land of the living race
I often forget I'm not saved by my works
but by God's Amazing Grace

Hush Anxious Thoughts

Hush anxious thoughts
I want to quiet my mind
The demands of your intrusiveness
Seems to take up all my time
My thoughts are all tangled
But I just want to unwind
Through the maze of my mind
I got to find a way out somehow
I'll plow my way through
Doing the impossible
Proving doubt wrong

Accomplishing what
I never thought I could do
I'm facing you bolding anxiety
I bet you don't have a clue
How I'm even standing up to you
I asked the Lord to help me to be strong
So I won't draw back in fear or defeat
Then we were able to collide
Oh, my thoughts and me

I won because I didn't listen
to the enemy inside my mind
But the Spirit within me that
was created to shine
The same Spirit that raised
Jesus up on the third day
When victory was won
Then my thoughts came
into alignment intertwining
with the Only Begotten Son

The 3:16 Promise

When I'm running on "empty"
Those powerful words in red speaks to me
The epitome of who I'm supposed to be constantly
reminds me
I'm more than just a prototype

I'm a reflection of Christ and by
His spirit I shine bright to where
I'm on the edge of a breakthrough
I've always been a Gem,
just hidden in plain sight

I'm more than just a product of my environment
I am a product of the sacrament of Christ
The Holy Spirit dwells within
And is my connection to eternal life

More Abundantly

John 10:10 speaks to me so clear
From the depths of my soul
I know God is all around
Supplying abundant life
Which means devil you can't have my life
Because I am the bride of Christ
Nor take away my joy
Attempting to steal what's rightfully mine
Nor destroy the plans of the Divine
My life has been written in stone
before the hands of time
God, I Thank You
for The Lamb's Book of Life

ℐ Just Gotta

Be free from the opinion of man
Be free of secretly wishing
that people would understand me
What is this person going to think,
what is that person going to say

Be free from allowing every little
interruption to dictate my day
Be free to make every "bad thing" work for me
Whether it's overthinking or anxiety
I'm going to let it out and turn it into poetry

Be free to write from my pain, knowing
that my experiences won't ever be the same
Because I've already won the battle
when I decided to use my writing as a healthy gain

A gain to bring others clarity that they are not lone
Seeing that my writing has a tone
A tone of freedom even in the danger zone
The danger zone of the mind that seems
to hold back the hands of time

Paddling through the waves of depression
Oh how I thank Jesus for making intercession
For me according to Romans 8:34
I know He is always standing at the door of my heart
Knowing what I'm thinking about
speaking before I even start

The Vault of the Sky

Daybreak signals the birds of
the air to make a joyful noise
From their nests among the
Branches of the trees of the Lord
The sky teaches us to serve the Lord
with gladness whether it's day or night
Genesis 1:1-31 focuses on God's Creation

God calls our body back to dust then
our spirit takes full form
An unparalleled reunion with God
Unabated praise singing with
the Angels of Heaven

Giving thanksgiving to God the Father
A praise worthy to the Most High
A sacrifice of His precious Son Jesus
that made it possible for us to unite as one

Battle Ready

When our mind is at war and in constant battle
We may have thoughts to draw
the sword on ourselves

But we have to keep looking up to the
Lighthouse that leads us back to shore
We are no longer in a slumber
even when we're awake

Our soul has been freed from a sleeping state
If put under trial, we wear Truth like a fitted belt
Truth is the key to set all free
Grace and mercy are our garments

Love is our royal crown
Our feet are established in peace
Faith is the shield that helps us see that
Truth, righteousness, peace, love, forgiveness,
salvation and prayer is right within our reach
And this is how You and I
will stand firm until the end

www.ingramcontent.com/pod-product-compliance
Lightning Source LLC
Chambersburg PA
CBHW060857120626
46553CB00001B/122